COMPANIES LIMITED BY GUARANTEE

COMPANIES LIMITED BY GUARANTEE

Elizabeth West
Solicitor, Manches

JORDANS
2000

Published by
Jordan Publishing Limited
21 St Thomas Street
Bristol BS1 6JS

British Library Cataloguing-in-Publication Data
A catalogue record for this book is available from the British Library.

ISBN 0 85308 638 9

Typeset by Mendip Communications Ltd, Frome, Somerset
Printed by MPG Books Ltd, Bodmin, Cornwall

PREFACE

The majority of company law textbooks are directed at the company limited by shares. There is very often a mention of the company limited by guarantee in the introductory chapter, explaining the different types of company that may be formed under the Companies Acts, but without addressing any of the questions of law peculiar to the company limited by guarantee. This is not helpful to those who manage or advise companies limited by guarantee, and this book aims to provide a comprehensive guide to company law as it affects companies limited by guarantee of all types.

The appendices contain a precedent for the self-contained memorandum and articles of association of a not-for-profit company limited by guarantee which is not to be registered as a charity or with any other special status. There are additional clauses including an objects clause and articles for a property management company, a procedure for expulsion of a member, and other precedent documents which may be useful in running a company limited by guarantee.

This book does not deal with insolvent companies limited by guarantee, and neither does it include any detailed or comprehensive coverage of direct or indirect taxation. It is not written with the concerns of any particular type of company limited by guarantee in mind, although some of the legal issues affecting charities, registered social landlords, insurance companies and trade associations are addressed in the first chapter and throughout the remaining chapters. Some of the propositions stated are necessarily speculative, in the absence of any supporting cases, meaning that a deduction has to be made from cases involving companies limited by shares or general principles of law.

There are references throughout this book to the 'Company Law Review'. This is a substantial review of major aspects of company law being undertaken by the Department of Trade and Industry's Company Law and Investigations Directorate. Its scope includes the formation of companies, directors' duties, and communications between members and the company. At the time of writing, the public consultation exercise is still under way, and the comments in this book about the likely outcome of the Review are based upon the recommendations of the Steering Group as set out in the various consultation papers issued to date. It is proposed that the Government will issue a White Paper in 2001 to outline the proposed reforms on the basis of the outcome of the Review.

For the sake of simplicity, 'he' is used to include 'he or she' throughout this book.

I should like to thank all my colleagues at Manches who have helped me in preparing this book, in particular Peter Angel, Richard Frost, Lorraine Morris and Julian Taylor.

ELIZABETH WEST
Manches, Oxford
August 2000

CONTENTS

Chapter 6   CAPITAL, DISTRIBUTIONS AND WINDING UP

TABLE OF CASES

References are to paragraph numbers.

TABLE OF STATUTES

References are to paragraph numbers; *italic* **numbers are to Appendix material.**

TABLE OF STATUTORY INSTRUMENTS

References are to paragraph numbers.

TABLE OF EUROPEAN LEGISLATION

References are to paragraph numbers.

TABLE OF ABBREVIATIONS

AGM	Annual General Meeting
ASA	Advertising Standards Authority
EGM	Extraordinary General Meeting
ICOM	Industrial Common Ownership Movement Limited
IOD	Institute of Directors
P & I	protection and indemnity
Table A	Companies (Tables A to F) Regulations 1985, SI 1985/805, Table A
'the Act'	Companies Act 1985 (as amended)

Chapter 1

THE NATURE AND PURPOSES OF A COMPANY LIMITED BY GUARANTEE

1.1 WHAT IS A COMPANY LIMITED BY GUARANTEE?

A company limited by guarantee is a private company in which the liability of the members is limited. The limit is set out in the memorandum of association of the company, and applies where the company is wound up and the company does not have sufficient funds to meet all the claims of its creditors. This guarantee can be for any amount per member, but it is common for the limit to be a nominal sum, typically £1 or £10. Most companies limited by guarantee do not have shares.[1] As at October 1998, there were 39,953 companies limited by guarantee registered at Companies House, excluding dormant and dissolved companies and those in liquidation or receivership.[2]

A company limited by guarantee is a suitable vehicle for a wide range of activities. Charities which are to have a corporate form must be companies limited by guarantee and must prevent the distribution of profit to their members, as must registered social landlords or housing associations. Companies limited by guarantee are also frequently used for the not-for-profit promotion of education, commerce, art, science or sport, or for promoting the interests of a particular section of society, or for promoting a particular policy.[3] They may also be used for managing semi-governmental and regulatory functions, including where a former governmental or local authority function has been privatised.

A substantial number of companies limited by guarantee are property management companies, set up to manage blocks of flats or estate developments. Mutual assurance companies may be formed as companies limited by guarantee, as may both members' clubs and proprietary clubs, the latter being a type of club where the owner of a business forms a club for its customers. Finally, clubs of traders and other companies may form themselves into a trade association with corporate form.

---

1   Companies limited by guarantee and having a share capital are dealt with at **1.9** below.
2   Source: *Developing the Framework: A Consultation Document From the Company Law Review Steering Group* March 2000, URN 00/656, p 293.
3   Organisations which exist to promote a particular section of society may benefit from particular exemptions in the anti-discrimination legislation: see Sex Discrimination Act 1975, ss 12, 34, and 43; Race Relations Act 1976, ss 11, 25 and 34; Disability Discrimination Act 1995, s 10.

The specific issues relevant to each type of organisation are discussed briefly in this chapter.

1.2 WHAT ARE THE ADVANTAGES OF INCORPORATION AS A COMPANY?

1.2.1 Separate legal personality

'Separate legal personality' means that the company can enter into contracts in its own name and can hold property in its own name. The members' rights to the property of the company are determined by company law and by the terms of the memorandum and articles of association of the company, but the members do not hold the legal title to the property, and do not have to get involved in every dealing with that property. It also means that the company can sue and be sued in its own name.

1.2.2 Limited liability

The members of a limited company are only liable to contribute the amount they have committed to the company; in the case of a company limited by guarantee this is equal to the amount of the guarantee, as set out in the memorandum. If a person sues the company and is awarded a sum of money (whether this is a simple debt or an award of damages), the creditor cannot enforce the order against the assets of the members. Neither can the company (unless the member agrees in writing) increase the amount of the guarantee or alter any other provision in the memorandum or articles which requires the member to pay money to the company.[1]

1.2.3 Perpetual succession

'Perpetual succession' is a consequence of separate legal personality. Since the company's assets are held in the company's name, no transfer of assets is required when a person involved in the company (either as member or as director) leaves and a new person joins.

1.2.4 Borrowing is made easier

Corporations can create 'floating charges' over their assets, which means that a creditor can secure a loan made to the company without hindering the use of the assets on which the loan is secured. A floating charge over the assets of a borrower will invariably be required by a bank lender. Unincorporated organisations can create floating charges but they would require registration under the Bills of Sale Acts.[2]

---

1   Companies Act 1985, s 16(1)(b).
2   Bills of Sale Act 1878 and Bills of Sale Act (1878) Amendment Act 1882.

1.2.5   Framework of company law

Although there is a substantial body of law which applies to unincorporated associations and trusts, it is not readily accessible because it is not found in a single statute, but is a combination of statutory provisions and case-law. The law of partnership is based on the Partnership Act 1890 but is frequently overruled by the terms of the partnership deed. Company law is not completely codified: for example, much of the law relating to directors' duties is not set out in the Companies Acts;[1] but the day-to-day detail of company law is set out in the Companies Act 1985 (as amended) and can answer many questions which may not be dealt with in the company's constitution. The framework of company law provides a ready-made system of checks and balances in the relationship between the company, its members and its officers.

1.3   THE DISADVANTAGES OF INCORPORATION

1.3.1   Registration

The company must be registered at Companies House[2] and certain changes must also be registered. An initial registration charge of £20 (or £100 in the case of a company to be created in a single day) is made; there are also charges for transactions such as the registration of a change of name. However, these costs have dramatically reduced over the years and they may reduce further as the registration process becomes more automated and increased computerisation makes Companies House more profitable.

The constitution of the company is contained in two documents: the memorandum of association and the articles of association, usually abbreviated to 'the memorandum and articles'. These two documents, and any resolutions passed by the company making changes to them, must be registered at Companies House, where they are publicly available. This means that any member of the public can, at a small cost, read and obtain copies of the rules which govern the operation of the company. If there are particular reasons for keeping some matters relating to the constitution of the company secret, these matters may be dealt with by means of by-laws if this is permitted in the registered constitution. The details of the rights attaching to a class of membership must, however, be registered, whether or not they are contained in the memorandum and articles.[3]

Details of directors' home addresses must also be registered at Companies House, together with other personal details and lists of their other directorships. The home address of the company secretary must also be

---

1   Although there may be a statutory statement of directors' duties as a result of the Company Law Review, see **4.5**.
2   The Registrar of Companies, or the Registrar of Companies for Scotland.
3   See Companies Act 1985, s 129 and **3.11**.

registered. Details of the members of the company (other than the first members who subscribe to the memorandum and articles on incorporation) do not have to be registered in the case of a company limited by guarantee without a share capital.

A checklist of the documents required for incorporation of a company limited by guarantee is set out at Appendix B.

1.3.2 Filing requirements

The Companies Act 1985 requires that details of changes in the board of directors must be registered at Companies House.

An annual return, in standard form, must also be filed every year and a fee of £15 paid. There are strict rules on the content and auditing of accounts, although many companies limited by guarantee will be able to take advantage of the audit exemption rules and the rules which allow small companies to file simplified accounts.

1.3.3 Restrictions on names

A company does not have absolute freedom in its choice of name.[1] The Companies Act 1985 requires publicity for the full name of the company in a number of circumstances and there are rules as to the content of the company's letterheaded notepaper.[2]

1.4 WHY USE A COMPANY LIMITED BY GUARANTEE?

1.4.1 Admission of members

The distinction between a company limited by shares and a company limited by guarantee is particularly significant in terms of the way in which members join and leave the company. Where the membership of a company is akin to membership of a club, a company limited by guarantee may be the most appropriate form of corporate structure. The admission and expulsion of members is dealt with by provisions in the articles. In contrast, in a company limited by shares the relevant principles are found in a combination of the articles, the Companies Acts, the common law applicable to companies and any shareholders' agreement.

Membership of a company limited by guarantee may be made to run in parallel with some other relationship. For example, in a property management company, the membership of the company is usually inextricably linked to the tenancy of one of the properties.[3] In a trade association,

---

1 See Chapter 2.
2 See **4.2.2** and Appendix E.
3 See Appendix A1.

membership can be linked to participation in a particular occupation or trade, or to the possession of a particular qualification. In a charity, the membership will usually consist simply of people who are interested in supporting the particular charitable object, and may, in practice, be confined to the members of the trustee body.

The constitution of a company limited by guarantee and not having a share capital will omit any references to the issue and transfer of shares, and so may be much simpler and easier to understand. This is important where the company is to have a widely-drawn membership, for example, where an existing club incorporates. In future, the requirements for the content of the constitution may be simplified further by the implementation of the recommendations of the Company Law Review.[1]

1.4.2   Changes in membership

The simplicity of the procedures for changing the membership of the company means that there are considerable advantages in choosing a company limited by guarantee for any corporate body where the members have motives other than investment. In a company limited by shares, if a prospective member wishes to join, he will have to subscribe for shares in the company, and, under the current law, the shares may not be issued at less than par (nominal) value.[2] It would be possible for a club or similar organisation to form itself as a company limited by shares and issue penny shares at par value. A large authorised share capital would be required in order to allow for expansion of the membership, and the articles would have to remove the statutory rights of pre-emption which apply to new issues of shares and require them first to be offered to existing shareholders.[3]

However, the disadvantages of using a company limited by shares are found in the mechanism which would be required to cope with members leaving the company or even being expelled. Shares cannot be cancelled except with the consent of the court. They can be bought back by the company, but only by following the detailed procedure set out in the Companies Act 1985,[4] and this would not be practicable as a means of dealing with a normal regular turnover of membership, although it could be used if there were to be a major reorganisation of the corporate structure. Redeemable shares could be issued, provided that there were some shares which were not redeemable,[5] but the date of redemption would need to be fixed in the articles. This would not create a flexible method for dealing with members' resignations. More likely would be a requirement that when a member resigned his membership, another member would have to buy his shares, or

1   See **2.1**.
2   No par value shares were capable of being created in the articles of a company until 1901.
3   Companies Act 1985, ss 89–96.
4   Part V, Chapter VII of the Companies Act 1985.
5   Companies Act 1985, s 159(2).

they would have to be transferred into a holding trust or other similar entity. This would not, however, remove the voting rights previously attached to the shares, and so some provision would have to be included in the articles to accommodate the suspension of the rights attaching to the 'floating' shares. Even if the membership were to be large enough and transient enough so that a prospective member could always be found to replace a retiring member, each retiring member would have to sign a stock transfer form. The directors would then have to approve the transfer and, normally, a share certificate would be issued.

In the case of a company limited by guarantee, a new member would simply apply for membership in whatever form was required by the articles, and the board (or admission committee) would admit him. Alternatively, the articles may provide for membership to be transferable.[1] No pre-emption rights apply; and when the member leaves, the fact is simply noted in the register of members. Any financial issues such as a refund of subscription are a matter of contract,[2] whether this is the contract formed by the articles or by some extrinsic contract.

1.4.3 Other advantages of a company limited by guarantee

A company limited by guarantee may be entitled to charitable grants or awards from public funds to which a company limited by shares would not be entitled. However, the terms of each individual grant-maker will need to be studied – in some cases the grant-maker will require that the company should be registered as a charity or that it should have a prohibition in its constitution on the distribution of profits to the company's members. There may also be intangible benefits in terms of the relationship with the members of the company where the not-for-profit clauses are included: the value to a member of participation in the company is not a financial one, but is represented by the right to vote and to participate in the making of policy (either directly, or by the election of the board of directors).

1.5 DISADVANTAGES OF A COMPANY LIMITED BY GUARANTEE

1.5.1 Lack of working capital

Although many companies limited by guarantee are very profitable as they retain trading profits over the years, the initial membership does not normally, as in the case of a company limited by shares, provide working capital by subscribing for shares in the company. Any contributions by the

---

1   In the case of a trade association, this may be important to the members and from the
    point of view of competition law (see **3.3**).
2   See **2.10**; unless on the facts the payment was a contribution to capital: see **6.2**.

members do not normally amount to an investment,[1] although it is not the fact of incorporation as a company limited by guarantee that prevents the distribution of dividends.[2] It is likely, however, that unless the members are convinced that any financial contributions that they make to the company will result in immediate and substantial benefits, they will be unwilling to contribute working capital to the company. Particularly in the early stages of a company, therefore, the company may be reliant on loan finance. A company limited by guarantee cannot, of course, raise funds from the public by means of a flotation on the Stock Exchange and a company limited by guarantee cannot be re-registered as a company limited by shares.

1.5.2 Difficulties with group structures

Complicated group structures may not be practical in the case of a company limited by guarantee. A company limited by guarantee can be registered with a single member which may itself be a company, if this is permitted by the articles. In other words, a company limited by guarantee may be a wholly-owned subsidiary of another company. Having separate legal personality, a company limited by guarantee can, if its constitution gives it the power to do so, hold shares in another company or be a member of another company limited by guarantee. However, groups involving companies limited by guarantee may not have the same tax treatment as a group of companies limited by shares. For example, in the case of *South Shore Mutual Insurance Co Ltd v Blair (Inspector of Taxes)*[3] the Special Commissioners of the Inland Revenue upheld a decision that group relief did not apply in the case of companies limited by guarantee. Group relief enables one member of a group of companies to surrender its tax losses so as to benefit another member of the group with taxable profits. However, the relief is drafted with companies limited by shares in mind: 75% of the ordinary share capital of one of the companies must be owned by the other, or a third company must own 75% of the share capital of the surrendering company and the claimant company. The Special Commissioners refused to give a wide interpretation to the phrase 'issued share capital', even though the practice of the Inland Revenue in the past had been to allow the group relief claim in the group in question; and held that because the company did not have shares it could not have an issued share capital and was not, therefore, eligible for the relief.

---

1   The articles can provide for the transfer of membership and the levying of membership
     fees.
2   See **2.6** and Chapter 6.
3   [1999] STC (SCD) 296.

1.6 OTHER POSSIBLE FORMS OF ORGANISATION

1.6.1 Friendly societies

Friendly societies are mutual societies funded by subscriptions from their members, which may have corporate form but are not companies. They are governed by the Friendly Societies Act 1992 and are supervised by the Friendly Societies Commission. They must have as their objects the provision of insurance or the provision of benefits for members if they become sick or unemployed, or the provision of funeral benefits.

1.6.2 Industrial and provident societies

Industrial and provident societies are generally co-operative societies and housing associations, although they may conduct any business or industry or trade on a co-operative basis or for the benefit of the community as a whole. They may also have charitable objects and, if they do, they are charities exempt from registration under the Charities Act 1993. They have corporate form but are not companies; they are governed not by the Companies Acts but by the Industrial and Provident Societies Acts 1965, 1967, 1975 and 1978.

1.6.3 Unincorporated associations

The main advantage of an unincorporated association or club is that there is no requirement that accounts and returns be filed at a public registry and only the club's constitution dictates the content of the accounts and the requirement to present them to the membership. The club's constitution will have much in common with the articles of association of a company; it will deal with admission to membership, the election of the club officers, and the conduct of meetings. However, the club itself is not a legal entity, which means that the property of the club must be held on trust, usually by the officers; and the members do not have the benefit of limited liability. A club is not, therefore, a suitable form of structure for any organisation which is to hold a substantial amount of non-cash property or is to enter into contracts with outsiders or provide goods or services to the public. It may be the most appropriate structure for an organisation with limited activity, such as a club for the former members of a school or college, or a sports and social club. Unincorporated associations may be charities.

1.6.4 Trusts

Where property is to be held for one or more specific purpose, it may be appropriate for a trust to be declared of that property. This means that two or more persons hold the property which is to be used only for those specific purposes and which is subject to the law of trusts. A trust may be charitable or private; in the case of private trusts, the beneficiaries must be identifiable by name or by class when the trust is set up. A trust is likely to be an appropriate form of entity if it is established only as a means of holding the title to a piece of land or other property, or where its only activity is the receipt and distribution of money. If it is intended that the organisation will conduct any form of commercial activity, it is more likely that a corporate form would be appropriate. A company also has the advantage that if there is a change of trustee, the property does not have to be transferred from the old trustee to the new trustee: the legal title to a trust's property is held by the trustees whereas the company holds the property in its own name. Charitable trusts can, however, have incorporated trustee bodies.[1]

1.6.5 Partnerships

A partnership is a collection of individuals or companies who agree to operate a business together, but which does not have corporate status and which does not have to register its constitution. It is primarily designed as a mechanism for the pooling of profit and is unlikely to be a realistic alternative to a company limited by guarantee. A partnership may not have more than 20 members[2] unless it comes within one of the exceptions defined by regulations; these include partnerships of solicitors and accountants. In a partnership, the liability of the partners is generally unlimited; although limited liability partnerships, a new type of legal entity, are being introduced. Limited liability partnerships will combine the flexibility of a partnership with the protection of limited liability, subject to certain safeguards for outsiders dealing with them, including provision for the public disclosure of financial and other information, and provisions applying on insolvency. Again, however, the primary function of the partnership is profit pooling.

1.7   TYPES OF COMPANY LIMITED BY GUARANTEE

1.7.1 Charities

A company is also a charity if it has objects which are charitable in law. The definition of charitable objects is not found in the Charities Acts, but rather in a collection of cases deriving from the preamble to a statute of Elizabeth I. Briefly, charitable objects are the relief of poverty, the advancement of education, the advancement of religion and other purposes beneficial to the community. A company whose objects are charitable is under a duty to register as a charity unless it is exempt from registration under the Charities Act 1993. A list of exempt charities is given in Sch 2 to the Charities Act 1993. Charities that do not hold land or have a permanent

---

1   See Part VII of the Charities Act 1993.
2   Companies Act 1985, s 716.

endowment and whose income does not exceed £1,000 per year are also exempt from registration.

Registered charities are subject to the supervisory jurisdiction of the Charity Commissioners and must make annual reports and accounts (subject to certain financial limits) which are put on the public record. Certain changes to the constitution of a charity require the consent of the Charity Commissioners before they can be put into effect.[1] Those concerned in the management of the charity (typically but not exclusively the directors of the company) are charity trustees and are subject to a range of duties and responsibilities, in addition to the requirements of company law.

1.7.2 Trade associations

A trade association is a body of persons formed for the purpose of furthering the trade interests of its members, or of persons represented by its members. It may or may not have a corporate structure. If the primary function of a trade association is the mutual benefit of its members, rather than the generation of profit, a company limited by guarantee is a suitable form of corporate structure.

The functions of trade associations include:

– the creation of codes of practice and standards;
– the creation of standard terms and conditions;
– the sharing of information, research, legal advice and training;
– the provision of a forum for discussion and lobbying of government; and
– the provision of public and employee relations services.

In the UK, the Office of Fair Trading has a duty to encourage the formulation of codes of practice, in the interests of those who deal with the trade association's members. However, the activities of trade associations can contravene competition law, both in the UK and in the European Union. Since the enactment of the Competition Act 1998, UK competition law has moved towards the format of European competition law: in particular, Articles 81 and 82 of the EC Treaty (as amended) are closely followed in the text of the Chapter I and Chapter II prohibitions in the Competition Act 1998, banning anti-competitive agreements and abuse of a dominant market position respectively. Competition aspects of trade associations are discussed further in Chapter 3.

When drafting the objects clause of the memorandum of a trade association, it is important to avoid inadvertently creating a trade union. The Trade Union and Labour Relations (Consolidation) Act 1992, s 1 provides that a trade union is an organisation which consists wholly or mainly of workers of one or more descriptions and whose principal purposes include

---

1   See **2.8** and **2.11**.

the regulation of relations between workers of that description(s) and employers or employers' associations. For this reason, the memorandum of a company limited by guarantee will sometimes state that the objects of the company will not extend to the regulation of relations between workers and employers.

1.7.3   Quasi-governmental functions

Companies limited by guarantee may be used as the corporate structure for many forms of self-regulatory or semi-governmental functions. Examples include the Advertising Standards Authority (ASA), the Training and Enterprise Councils, privatised governmental authorities and the companies operating in the internet infrastructure. One question which arises is whether, in terms of the remedies available to an outsider dealing with these organisations, they should be treated as private law bodies (because a company is a creature of private law) or as public law bodies, owing to the nature of their functions. In particular, should their decisions be susceptible to applications for judicial review?

It is a long-established principle of law that the decisions of public bodies may be judicially reviewed. Typically, the cases involve a body with powers conferred on it by statute which has failed to observe an express procedural requirement or has failed to comply with the rules of natural justice.[1] The applicability of the principles of judicial review to self-regulatory bodies was considered in the case of *R v City Panel on Takeovers and Mergers ex p Datafin plc*.[2] The City Panel was an unincorporated association set up by City institutions to promote a code of conduct applying to listed companies involved in takeovers and mergers, and to decide whether in particular cases there had been a breach of the rules in the code. In the *Datafin* case, Sir John Donaldson said that the term 'self-regulation' described the situation where 'a group of people, acting in concert, use their collective power to force themselves and others to comply with a code of conduct of their own devising'. He reviewed the relevant cases and noted that it was clear that, in order for an organisation's decisions to be reviewable, there had to be some public element, typically found where the body is part of a regulatory system, or is non-statutory as a result of a government decision, or is supported by statutory powers and penalties. The court would not review decisions of bodies whose source of powers was wholly consensual. He was influenced in this case by the fact that the Panel had immense de facto control, and that transgressions of the code would be likely to be penalised by the Stock Exchange or by the Department for Trade and Industry; and concluded that the source of the Panel's powers was not merely consensual.

The test developed by the *Datafin* case has come to be summarised as: if the self-regulatory body did not exist, would Parliament have intervened in

---

1   See **3.9.3**.
2   [1987] 2 WLR 699.

order to regulate the activity? It is not always easy to reconcile the cases in which this test has been applied: in *R v Disciplinary Committee of the Jockey Club ex p Aga Khan*[1] a decision of the Jockey Club was held not to be judicially reviewable. However, in *R v Advertising Standards Authority ex p Insurance Services plc*[2] a decision of the ASA was held to be reviewable, following *Datafin*. An additional factor was that the role of the ASA was implicitly recognised in regulations implementing an EC Directive[3] requiring Member States to control misleading advertisements. As has been pointed out,[4] the test applied in these cases is not a reliable one, because the proper limits of legislative interference are not universally agreed upon. To put it another way, why should a court's decision as to whether to accept jurisdiction depend on a hypothesis as to Parliament's intentions? Courts are able to consider the intention of Parliament in construing a particular statutory provision, but that is not the same as presenting a hypothesis as to non-existent legislation. Lord Woolf has called[5] for a wider power to review the decisions of organisations who do not derive their powers from statute. He has proposed that the test should be whether the interest affected by the decision is adequately protected by private law. This would mean, presumably, that if the person complaining were a member of the organisation in question he would be expected to use the constitutional and company law remedies available to him, but an outsider affected by a decision of a private body which was not a matter of contract would be able to bring an action for judicial review.

The action for judicial review is not confined, in the context of a company limited by guarantee, to a review of the exercise of self-regulatory powers. In principle, any decision of a company limited by guarantee which is of a sufficiently public law nature will be susceptible to review. For example, in *R v Cobham Hall School, ex parte G*,[6] it was held that the administration by a private school, constituted as a company limited by guarantee, of its participation in the assisted places scheme, was a public function because it involved the application of public funds.

1.7.4 Mutual assurance companies

A mutual assurance company is an insurance company in which the members of the company are, effectively, both the insurer and the insured. Groups of interested parties may form companies to provide mutual assurance to cover risks for which cover is not available on the mainstream insurance market, or for which it is more convenient or economical to provide cover on a mutual basis, for example to cover professional

1   [1993] 2 All ER 853.
2   (1990) 2 Admin LR 77.
3   Council Directive 84/450 on Control of Misleading Advertisements.
4   S Fredman and G S Morris 'The Costs of Exclusivity: Public and Private Re-Examined' (1994) PL 69.
5   Woolf 'Judicial Review: A Possible Programme of Reform' (1992) PL 221.
6   (1997) *The Times*, 13 December.

negligence risks within a particular profession.[1] Mutual insurance companies are typically not-for-profit organisations in their operation and do not aim to generate a profit. Their constitutions will not, however, prohibit the distribution of profits to the members and it would be the members who would be entitled to any surplus on a winding up.

Protection and indemnity (P & I) clubs are a type of mutual assurance organisation for ship owners. They first appeared in the mid-nineteenth century, to fill gaps in the insurance protection offered by the traditional insurance market, and to provide indemnity for claims relating to the ships' cargoes. A member enters into a contract of insurance with the company in respect of a particular ship, but there is no insurance policy with a premium to pay. Instead, the members guarantee to pay each others' claims on a mutual basis, and 'calls' are made as necessary. The articles form the basis of the contract of insurance, supplemented by rules dealing with the risks covered. The articles also deal with the role of the board of directors (usually called the committee), who will deal with disputes between the members and review any claims, removing the need for any claims to be arbitrated.

The Insurance Companies Act 1982 requires all insurers to be companies or registered societies. Any person conducting insurance business must be registered under the Act unless he is exempt. Insurance business is not defined under the Insurance Companies Act 1982 and, therefore, any activity of a company limited by guarantee may be covered by the 1982 Act if it provides monetary benefits in the event that identified risks occur, whether or not the company has under its memorandum the power to provide the benefit. Exemptions include Lloyd's of London, registered friendly societies, and trade unions and employers' organisations providing provident or strike benefits to their own members. Note that the definition of 'insurance company' for the purposes of the Companies Act 1985 covers any company which carries on insurance business in common with any other business or businesses.[2]

The directors are under the same duties as the directors of any other company, but in addition must be fit and proper persons to act as directors of an insurance company, and the company's affairs must be conducted in a sound and prudent manner, with adequate accounting records being maintained and adequate systems being used to control the company's business and its accounting records.[3] There are special provisions relating to the accounts of insurance companies and also detailed rules which apply on a winding up.

.

---

1   Or, as in the *South Shore* case (see footnote 3 on p 17), the insurance of amusement parks at Blackpool.
2   Companies Act 1985, s 720(5).
3   Insurance Companies Act 1982, s 5(4) and Sch 2A.

1.7.5   Property management companies

Property management companies are set up by the freeholder or head leaseholder of a piece of land in order to hold the title to, and sometimes to manage, parts of an estate or block of flats which are to be owned jointly by all the tenants. The tenants will be the members of the company, and they will elect directors, although the activities of the company (for example, the maintenance of the common parts) will often be contracted back to the freeholder. When a tenant sells his property, he will be required to resign from the company (or the articles may provide for resignation to be automatic in those circumstances) and the new tenant will be admitted to the company.[1]

Some property management companies are companies limited by shares. Each of the tenants will take one share in the company. The first shareholders will have to pay at least the nominal value of the shares, or accept the liability to pay the nominal value if the directors require it, as shares cannot be issued at below the nominal value. The shares can, however, have a nominal value of one penny. When a tenant wishes to sell his property, he must also transfer his share in the company to the incoming tenant. This will require the old tenant to sign a stock transfer form (and if the share is not fully paid, the new tenant will have to sign the stock transfer as well). If one of the units is to remain empty for a length of time, someone will need to be found to hold the former tenant's share as shares cannot (except by following a procedure which is too complicated to be appropriate for this situation) be transferred back to the company or cancelled.

In contrast, in the case of a company limited by guarantee, if a unit is to remain empty the former tenant will simply resign his membership of the company (or the articles may be drafted so as to provide for automatic termination of membership on surrendering or transferring the tenancy), and the new tenant, when there is one, will be admitted. There is no paperwork which needs to be completed between the old and the new tenants.

The role of property management companies may change if Parliament approves proposals to reform the leasehold laws, introduced in the Queen's speech at the opening of Parliament in November 1999.[2] A system of commonhold is proposed, similar to that existing in the United States and in Australia, together with a system of collective enfranchisement. However, it can be expected that existing freeholders will put up a great deal of resistance to the new legislation.

---

1   See the Companies House Guidance Notes: *Flat Management Companies*, available on the
    website www.companieshouse.gov.uk.
2   This is not likely to be before the 2000/01 Parliamentary session.

1.7.6   Registered social landlords

Registered social landlords are bodies established to provide low cost housing and hostels, registered under the Housing Act 1996. Their activities are supervised by the Housing Corporation, a 'quango' regulated by the 1996 Act. They may be unincorporated housing associations registered as charities, industrial and provident societies or companies. Industrial and provident societies are exempt charities if their objects are charitable; companies may be charitable but if so they must register with the Charity Commissioners as well as at Companies House. If a registered social landlord is a company, it is likely to be a company limited by guarantee, since even if its activities are non-charitable the Housing Act 1996 requires it to be a not-for-profit organisation. The Act also contains restrictions on the objects that may be included in the memorandum of a registered social landlord,[1] and in the activities that the company may carry out in support of the objects.[2] The National Housing Federation has a useful website listing publications for sale.[3]

Registered social landlords are subject to restrictions under the Housing Act 1996 and circulars of the Housing Corporation. In particular, changes to the memorandum and articles will require the consent of the Housing Corporation as well as compliance with the Companies Act 1985 procedure. Benefits provided to board members, like benefits to charity trustees, are strictly controlled, as are benefits to members and their families.[4]

If the company is also a charity there will be three sets of rules to comply with: company law; charity law; and the Housing Act 1996. The restrictions imposed by charity law presented a problem for registered social landlords which bought former council houses whose tenants would not all qualify as charitable beneficiaries. However, the reduction in government grants given to compensate for corporation tax charged now provide an additional incentive for registered social landlords to become charities.

1.7.7   Scientific research associations

Scientific research associations are associations of two or more persons, given special tax status[5] if their objects are confined to the undertaking of scientific research which may lead to an extension of trade. Scientific research associations may be companies limited by guarantee, and the memorandum of the company must contain a prohibition on the distribution of profits to the members. Approval of scientific research association status is in practice given by the Department of Trade and Industry.[6]

---

1   Housing Act 1996, s 2.
2   Housing Act 1996, s 2 and SI 1996/2256, SI 1999/985 and SI 1999/1206.
3   www.housing.org.uk.
4   Housing Act 1996, Sch 1.
5   Under Income and Corporation Taxes Act 1988, s 508.
6   By the SME Technology Directorate.

1.8 A HISTORY OF COMPANIES LIMITED BY GUARANTEE

The company limited by guarantee is not as old as company law. Many educational institutions were incorporated by Royal Charter or by statute, as were trade associations which in many cases took the place of the medieval guilds. Modern equivalents of these companies could equally be formed as companies limited by guarantee. Trade unions, in contrast, were not given corporate status as they were regarded as unlawful in principle and, in fact, were restrained as much as possible. No doubt if companies limited by guarantee had been invented as the legal structure for trade unions the relevant principles of company law would have been further developed by additional case-law to the benefit of all companies limited by guarantee.

Joint stock companies existed from the early eighteenth century but it was only following the failure of the South Sea investment scheme that Parliament began to take an interest in the regulation of corporations. The Bubble Act was designed to ensure that no body corporate could issue shares without authority given by a Royal Charter or by an Act of Parliament. This was easily evaded by the mechanism of the deed of settlement company, in which the assets were held by trustees but the enterprise was managed by directors. In 1825 the Bubble Act was repealed and was later replaced by an Act to legalise the deed of settlement company, and for the first time a public registration requirement for companies was introduced. The concept of limited liability was not introduced until 1855. Until this time, the concept of members' rights had centred on the idea of corporate membership, as companies generally had small capital and tended to be financed by loan stock rather than raising equity capital.

The first Companies Act was passed in 1862 and was mainly a consolidation measure, following the numerous Companies Bills introduced in the late 1850s. However, s 9 of the 1862 Act introduced companies limited by guarantee for the first time, and brought banking and insurance companies under the same legislative umbrella. Section 23 of the Companies Act 1867 introduced the predecessor of what is now s 30 of the Companies Act 1985. An association not for profit and 'formed to promote commerce, art, science, religion, charity or other useful object' could be registered without the word 'limited' in its name provided it obtained the consent of the Board of Trade.

1.9   COMPANIES LIMITED BY GUARANTEE AND HAVING A SHARE CAPITAL

Before 22 December 1980 it was possible for a company to be formed with a share capital, but with the limit of liability being achieved by means of the guarantee in the memorandum. However, it is now no longer possible for new companies limited by guarantee with a share capital to be formed.[1] Companies limited by guarantee and having a share capital are still found today, and in legal terms are a hybrid, with certain of the principles applying to them as if they were a company limited by shares, and other principles applying from the rules relating to companies limited by guarantee. Only the latter principles are addressed in this book.

The member of a company limited by guarantee and having a share capital has, in fact, two distinct liabilities: he is liable to pay the sum due on his shares and also to contribute to the assets of the company if it is wound up, according to the guarantee in the memorandum.[2] The rules relating to maintenance of share capital will apply to a company limited by guarantee and having a share capital. This means that if a person ceases to be a member of the company he does not also automatically cease to be a shareholder. Unless the articles of the company so provide, there is no requirement that a member should become a shareholder, or that a person who has subscribed for shares should become a member.

Companies limited by guarantee and having a share capital cannot be registered today. Furthermore, s 15(2) of the Companies Act 1985 prevents a company limited by guarantee with a share capital being created in the form of a company limited by guarantee without a share capital. It provides that every provision in the memorandum or articles of association, or any provision in a resolution of a company limited by guarantee and not having a share capital, purporting to divide the company's undertaking into shares or interests is to be treated as a provision for share capital. This applies for the purposes of the provisions of the Act relating to the memorandum, and to s 1(4) of the Act.[3]

1.10   THE FUTURE OF COMPANIES LIMITED BY GUARANTEE

Companies limited by guarantee represent a significant part of the remaining mutual organisations in the UK. In the late twentieth century, many building societies and some mutual assurance organisations abandoned mutuality in the face of competitive pressures which led them to seek

---

1   Companies Act 1985, s 1(4).
2   See **2.7**.
3   The construction of s 15(2) of the Companies Act 1985 was considered in *South Shore Mutual Insurance Co Ltd v Blair (Inspector of Taxes)* [1999] STC (SCD) 296.

capital funding from the public by means of 'conversion' to public limited companies and flotation on the Stock Exchange. It may have been only a matter of historical accident that they were originally formed as mutual organisations and not as companies limited by shares, since as we have seen, the concept of limited liability of a company was not introduced until the second half of the nineteenth century. The fact that mutual organisations fulfilling particular functions have in many cases demutualised does not mean that there is no future for the mutual organisation or the company limited by guarantee. Where the motives of the members remain mutual benefit or philanthropic, a company limited by guarantee remains the ideal form of entity to satisfy these motives.

The era of demutualisation has also seen the rise of a new social creature, the 'carpetbagger', who opens a building society account or takes out an insurance policy merely in order to become a member of the mutual society, in the hope of securing a windfall payment on conversion. Carpetbaggers have also sought to identify rich mutual organisations which can be 'invaded' and forced into demutualisation. This is particularly the case where the level of investment required in order to secure a vote at the general meeting of the company is relatively low – perhaps the placing of £1 in a share account, or the payment of a £10 annual membership fee. In many mutual organisations, it is open to any member to stand for election to the board of directors, perhaps with only one nomination required from a fellow member. The carpetbagger will use this mechanism as a method for putting the proposal for demutualisation to the company as a whole. In November 1999, the Treasury announced plans to introduce a new regime for the demutualisation of building societies and life insurance companies, increasing the level of support required and increasing the probation period before an investor becomes a member.

In any event, the carpetbagger should beware the company limited by guarantee. A building society may be converted by means of a resolution of 50% of the members, but changes to the constitution of a company require the approval of at least 75% of the members and if there is to be a transfer of assets to a new company, this is likely to entail a scheme which in addition requires the sanction of the court under Part XIII of the Companies Act 1985.[1] If the company has restrictions on distribution in its memorandum, these would need to be removed prior to the transfer of assets. The carpetbagger would also need to comply with the rules relating to the elections to the board in order to obtain support for his plan, or would need to rely on the provisions of the Companies Act 1985 concerning the requisitioning of meetings by members.[2]

The trend to conversion of the former mutuals might seem to be at odds with the idea of a 'stakeholder society'. The holders of shares in the new banks, for example, do not represent stakeholders, but rather investors

---

1   See **6.8**.
2   See **5.1.4**.

seeking profits. Even those former mutual members who have benefited from windfalls are likely to see their ownership of shares as unconnected with their interests as customers of the banks. However, the role for mutual organisations will be maintained and may even be strengthened in the stakeholder society. Clubs and trade associations, for example, may be able to offer stakeholder pensions when these are introduced.

Moreover, the idea of a mutual organisation fits other social trends: the development of the internet, for example, has in the UK been at least partially carried out by mutual organisations or trade associations representing businesses operating the internet infrastructure, in the absence of a statutory model.[1] The privatisation of public services, or 'externalisation', is also frequently achieved by the establishment of a company limited by guarantee, particularly where the externalised function is to be operated by a workers' co-operative established by former employees of the public body.[2]

These businesses seek to demonstrate that the function can be run efficiently and fairly in the private sector without the need for government supervision or regulation, but while maintaining a public ethos and without the profit motive overriding the commitment to public service. A company limited by guarantee, incorporating a ban on distribution of profits, represents a realistic compromise.

1.11   COMPANY LAW REFORM

A strategic consultation document issued in March 2000[3] addresses the key areas of governance of companies, and issues for small and private companies. No change is proposed in the law of companies limited by guarantee as such, but companies limited by guarantee may be affected by some aspects of the proposed reform in the area of corporate governance and the holding of meetings. It is recommended[4] that charitable companies should have their own form of incorporation, regulated by the Charity Commissioners, which would be more specifically attuned to the needs of charities and would remove the requirement to report to two regulators. The proposed name is the 'Charitable Incorporated Institution', abbreviated to CII. However, it is not proposed to extend the new type of legal entity to other types of not-for-profit company.

---

1   For example, Nominet UK, The London Internet Exchange Limited, The JNT Association, The Internet Society of England, The Internet Society of Scotland.
2   See, for example, the materials published by the Industrial Common Ownership Movement Limited (ICOM).
3   *Developing the Framework: A Consultation Document From the Company Law Review Steering Group*, March 2000, URN 00/656.
4   At least in the case of charities in England and Wales, as legislation on the creation of charities is a matter which has been devolved to the Scottish Parliament.

Chapter 2

THE MEMORANDUM AND ARTICLES

2.1 INTRODUCTION

The constitution of a company is contained in its memorandum and articles of association. These are two different documents and different rules apply to their interpretation; although they are commonly referred to together. The memorandum of association of a company ('the memorandum') governs the relationship between the company and the outside world, in terms of its purposes, powers, ability to distribute its capital and income, and the consequences of winding up. In contrast, the articles of association ('the articles') govern the detail of the relationship between the members and the procedures for calling meetings and electing the board. The Company Law Review[1] proposes that for new companies formed after its implementation, the distinction between the memorandum and articles should be abolished, but that existing companies should not be required to re-register. In an order proposed under the Electronic Communications Act 2000, it is proposed to enable documents for the formation of companies to be submitted to Companies House by electronic means and bearing electronic signatures.[2]

2.2 THE CONTENTS OF THE MEMORANDUM

2.2.1 The requirements of the Companies Act 1985, s 2

Section 2 of the Companies Act 1985 sets out what must be included in the memorandum. In common with other limited companies, a company limited by guarantee must include its name,[3] country of its registered office,[4] a statement of the objects for which it is established[5] and a statement that the liability of the members is limited. A company limited by guarantee must also include in its memorandum the statement of the amount of the guarantee as required by s 2(4) of the Act.[6]

---

1   *Modern Company Law for a Competitive Economy: the Strategic Framework (A Consultation Document from the Company Law Review Steering Group* February 1999, URN 99/654.
2   *Electronic Communications for Companies: An Order Under the Electronic Communications Bill (A Consultative Document)* February 2000 URN 00/626.
3   See **2.3**.
4   See **2.8.6**.
5   See **2.4**.
6   See **2.7**.

2.2.2 Table C

Regulations[1] contain a precedent for the memorandum of a company limited by guarantee, in Table C. Section 2 of the Companies Act 1985 states that the memorandum of a company limited by guarantee shall be; 'as near to that form as circumstances admit'. In practice, however, the memorandum in Table C is interpreted as representing only the general form or outline of the memorandum, and the promoters of a company limited by guarantee will usually draft a bespoke version which adds other elements.

The use of Table C was considered by Megarry J in *Gaiman v National Association for Mental Health*.[2] The case concerned the expulsion from membership of certain of the company's members, and one of the arguments put forward by the members was that the article that governed expulsion was not valid as it was not contained in Table C. Megarry J noted that there was no authority on the subject, and continued (at p 328, B–C):

> 'In my judgment, it is for the draftsman to mould his articles to the needs of the company as the promoters see it at the time. He should bear in mind what he finds in Table C, as well, of course, as the terms of the Act. But provided he follows the general form of the relevant table, setting out matters in numbered paragraphs and dividing the subject matter between the memorandum and articles in the manner suggested by the table, I cannot see why he should not be free to add, subtract or vary as the needs of the case suggest.'

2.2.3 The subscribers

The first members of a company are called the 'subscribers'. This terminology dates from the foundation of company law when incorporation was effected by executing a deed of settlement. It sometimes causes confusion where a company limited by guarantee is a club or trade association and members are required to pay a membership fee or subscription in order to maintain their membership. The memorandum must be signed by at least one subscriber in the presence of a witness.[3]

2.2.4 Single-member companies

If there is only one subscriber to the memorandum, and so only one member of the company, the Companies Act 1985 provides for the quorum at meetings of the single member to be one, regardless of what is said in the articles.[4] This replaces the usual rule that, in the absence of any express provision in the articles, a quorum is at least two members personally present.[5] However, this does not apply where there is more than one

---

1 Companies (Tables A to F) Regulations 1985, SI 1985/805.
2 [1971] Ch 317.
3 Companies Act 1985, s 2(6).
4 Companies Act 1985, s 370A.
5 Companies Act 1985, s 370(4).

member of the company. If the articles are to provide for the members, rather than the board, to have the power to admit more members,[1] care should be taken to ensure that the quorum specified is not greater than the initial number of members.[2]

2.3 THE COMPANY NAME

2.3.1 Choice of name

A company limited by guarantee has, in principle, the same choice of name as any other company, but in addition it may take advantage of s 30 of the Companies Act 1985 which in certain specified circumstances permits the company, although having the benefit of limited liability for its members, to be formed with a name that does not contain the word 'limited' or its Welsh equivalent 'cyfyngedig' (see below). Note that a company may be registered with the word 'limited' or its statutory abbreviation 'ltd' and, strictly speaking, the two are not interchangeable: the company's name ends with the form shown on the certificate of incorporation.

2.3.2 Business names

If the company has a place of business in Great Britain and carries on business in Great Britain under a name which does not consist of its corporate name (ie its registered name) or its corporate name with an addition merely to indicate that the business is carried on in succession to the former owner of the business, then it is subject to the Business Names Act 1985. This requires the corporate name to be stated (with an address for service), broadly, on all business stationery and at each place in Great Britain where the business is carried on. The Business Names Act 1985 also imposes the same restrictions in relation to names (see below) as the Companies Act 1985 does for corporate names.

2.3.3 Prohibited words

Section 26 of the Companies Act 1985 sets out the restrictions that apply to the names of all types of company. Those that apply to companies limited by guarantee are:

(1) 'limited' (or, if desired, 'cyfyngedig' in the case of a company whose registered office is to be in Wales) or their respective abbreviations must not appear except at the end of the name;
(2) the name must not be the same as any name appearing in the index of company names (s 26(3) of the Companies Act 1985 sets out certain factors, such as punctuation, which are to be disregarded by the registrar when applying this rule);

---

1   See Chapter 3.
2   See further **3.6.2** on single-member companies.

(3) the use of the name must not (in the opinion of the Secretary of State) constitute a criminal offence or be offensive;

(4) except with the approval of the Secretary of State (in practice, the registrar of companies), the name must not suggest that the company is connected with national or local government; and

(5) except with the approval of the relevant authority, the name must not include any word or expression specified in regulations made under s 29 of the Companies Act 1985 (see below).

2.3.4 Sensitive words and misleading names

Regulations[1] limit the use of certain words and expressions in the company's name. In some cases, there are criteria which the registrar will apply in deciding whether or not a company may be registered with a name containing the word or phrase. Examples of words in this category are: council, group, national, society and trust. In other cases, the promoters are required to obtain the consent of a specified government body or private institution as a condition of registration, and that body will ensure that the company conducts activities within the area suggested by the words and in accordance with particular rules or to particular standards. Examples of words in this second category are: charity, health centre, nursing and royal. In addition, there are some words which if used in the company's name, might constitute a criminal offence under separate legislation, such as: bank, drug, patent and veterinary.[2]

The Insolvency Act 1986 also prevents a director or shadow director of a company that has gone into insolvent liquidation from forming another company using a name that is the same as, or confusingly similar to, the liquidated company's name.[3]

2.3.5 Direction to change a company's name

The Secretary of State may direct a company to change its name if in his opinion the name 'gives so misleading an indication of the nature of its activities as to be likely to cause harm to the public'.[4] The company has the power to challenge the direction in court but this is subject to a time-limit of three weeks.[5]

---

1 Company and Business Names Regulations 1981, SI 1981/1685 as amended.
2 These are selected examples only, and readers should refer to Companies House Guidance Booklets GBF2 and GBF3 (available on the website www.companieshouse.gov.uk), or to Jordans' *Company and Business Names Sensitive Word Information Pack*.
3 Insolvency Act 1986, s 216.
4 Companies Act 1985, s 32(1).
5 Companies Act 1985, s 32(3).

This section was considered in a case concerning the Association of Certified Public Accountants.[1] The Association was aimed at individuals who call themselves accountants and offer accountancy services to the public but who have no formal accountancy qualifications and are not members of other associations of accountants. The Secretary of State contended that the name 'Certified' was confusing because it implied that the Association maintained a system for ensuring a level of professional qualification, standing and competence on the part of its members, which it did not. The court held that the procedure for challenge of the Secretary of State's direction was neither an appeal nor a procedure in the nature of judicial review. It was for the court to decide the matter afresh on the evidence presented to it by both sides, and considering the situation at the date of the judgment rather than the date of the direction. On the facts, 'Certified' was found to be likely to indicate to a substantial number of people that there was something objectively significant about the members' qualifications, training and experience; clients consult accountants expecting not only probity but also a level of expertise. They would pay more for the advice given by a 'certified' accountant and would therefore be harmed by the misleading name.

Jacob J also confirmed some principles of general application. It is not sufficient that the name is misleading; there must be a likelihood of harm: 'It is difficult to imagine harm, for instance, if a company called Robin Jacob (Fishmongers) Ltd in fact carried on a business of bookbinding.'[2] No specific instances of someone having been misled need be shown, and neither need an intention to mislead be shown, although these factors would be relevant evidence. 'Misleading' bears the same meaning as in trade mark and passing off cases in that it means 'misleading to at least a substantial number of people'.

Section 32(1) of the Companies Act 1985 applies only to the full company name and not to any trading names, abbreviations, or logos used by the company.

2.3.6 Names of charities

There are similar but more extensive restrictions applicable to the names of companies which are to be registered as charities. The Charity Commissioners have the power to direct a change of name of a registered charity whose name is the same as or, in their opinion, too like, an existing charity (whether or not that charity is registered).[3] The new name is chosen by the directors of the company but must be approved by the Charity

---

1   *Association of Certified Public Accountants of Britain v Secretary of State for Trade and Industry* [1998] 1 WLR 164, [1997] 2 BCLC 307, ChD.
2   [1997] 2 BCLC 307 at 310i.
3   Charities Act 1993, s 6(2)(a). Note that this power lasts only for a period of 12 months after registration: s 6(3).

Commissioners.[1] There are further powers which apply to registered and excepted charities (but not to exempt charities): the Charity Commissioners may direct a change of name if the name of the charity is in their opinion likely to mislead the public as to the stated objects of the charity or its activities;[2] note that there is no specific requirement (as in the case of the Companies Act equivalent) that the misleading nature should be likely to cause harm to the public.

There are also sensitive words which apply to charities, and the Charity Commissioners may direct a change of name if a sensitive word is used, or if the name of the charity misleadingly gives the impression that the charity is connected with government or a local authority 'or with any other body of persons or any individual'.[3] Finally, the Charity Commissioners have the power to direct a change of name if a charity's name is offensive.[4] Unlike the powers given in the Companies Act, the Charity Commissioners' powers do not apply before registration.

Where a change of name is directed, it is the directors of the company who must change the name of the company,[5] whereas a voluntary change of name is effected by a special resolution of the members of the company. The resolution of the directors changing the name of the company must be registered at Companies House,[6] and the change of name does not take effect until the Registrar issues the certificate of change of name.[7] Despite the compulsory nature of the change of name, the new name could still in principle contravene the Companies Act provisions on names and so care should be taken by the directors when selecting the new name.

2.3.7   Exemption from using the word 'limited'

The promoters of a company limited by guarantee may feel that the inclusion of the word 'limited' (or its Welsh equivalent, 'cyfyngedig') as part of the company's name is inappropriate where the company is set up to promote charitable or philanthropic objects. Although it is certainly not the case that a company describing itself as 'limited' is necessarily a commercial company, this may be the impression that is given to the public, and this may be felt to be inappropriate or misleading. In particular, the trustees of a company which is a charity seeking public donations may feel that the inclusion of the word 'limited' in the company name may deter potential benefactors.

The Companies Act 1985 contains provisions which meet this need. Section 30(3) sets out the requirements which must be satisfied before a company

---

1   Charities Act 1993, s 6(1).
2   Charities Act 1993, s 6(2)(b).
3   Charities Act 1993, s 6(2)(b) and (c).
4   Charities Act 1993, s 6(2)(e).
5   Charities Act 1993, s 6(4) and (8).
6   Companies Act 1985, s 380(4)(e).
7   Companies Act 1985, s 28(6).

with limited liability may register its name on formation or a change of name without including the word 'limited' or 'cyfyngedig':

'Those requirements are that –

(a) the objects of the company are (or in the case of a company about to be registered, are to be) the promotion of commerce, art, science, education, religion, charity or any profession, and anything incidental or conducive to any of those objects; and

(b) the company's memorandum or articles of association –

    (i) require its profits (if any) or other income to be applied in promoting its objects;

    (ii) prohibit the payment of dividends to its members, and

    (iii) require all the assets which would otherwise be available to its members generally to be transferred on its winding up either to another body with objects similar to its own or to another body the objects of which are the promotion of charity and anything incidental or conducive thereto (whether or not the body is a member of the company).'

There are some companies in existence without the word 'limited' or 'cyfyngedig' in their name but whose objects do not satisfy these requirements. This is because the companies legislation before the Companies Act 1981 came into force allowed any company to apply for dispensation from the requirement to use the word limited in their name, rather than setting out a general exemption.[1] Section 19 of the Companies Act 1948 required the licence of the Board of Trade for the omission of the word limited. There was a pro forma constitution, containing clauses designed for use by charities,[2] because the Board of Trade rarely approved an application by a non-charitable company unless it could show support from a government department or a chamber of commerce.

Section 30 does not require that the objects clause of the company be cast in the format of a specific object and then other things incidental or conducive to that object. It is intended to prevent a company from bringing itself within the section by including one of the permitted objects in amongst a more wide-ranging set of objects. Neither does the clause prevent the inclusion of the usual wide range of express powers.[3] It would not appear to be necessary for the company to follow the exact wording of the section in its objects clause, so that the test is whether the objects substantively come within the section. This is suggested by the fact that the section refers to the 'promotion of … any profession', which would rarely be used in that exact form in an objects clause.

---

1   See Companies Act 1985, s 30(2).
2   For example, there was a clause in the memorandum referring to property held on charitable trusts being subject to the jurisdiction of the Charity Commissioners.
3   See **2.5**.

A statutory declaration may be sworn[1] by a person named as director or secretary of the company in the statement delivered to the registrar of companies, or by a solicitor engaged in the formation of the company, that the section has been complied with. If such a declaration is provided, the Companies Act 1985 provides that the Registrar is entitled to assume that it is sufficient evidence of the matters stated in it.[2] Therefore, in practice, the onus of proving that the section applies is placed on the promoters of the company. The Companies Act 1985 also provides that the Secretary of State may direct a change of name to include the word 'limited' if it appears that the company has carried on any business other than the objects stated in s 30, has applied its profits other than in support of those objects, or has paid a dividend to any of its members.[3] The power to change the objects clause and other provisions of the memorandum and articles is also subject to the requirements of s 30 in the case of a company claiming the exemption.[4]

If s 30 applies, the company is exempt from the requirements of the Companies Act 1985 relating to the publication of the name, and from the requirements to deliver lists of its members to the Registrar.[5] Therefore, the section of the annual return form relating to past and present members of the company is omitted in the case of a s 30 company and the shuttle version of the form produced from the Companies House database will reflect this.

2.3.8   Trade mark infringement

The fact that a company name is accepted by Companies House does not mean that it can be used without infringing another person's registered trade mark, or without committing the tort of passing off. Business names used by companies may likewise lead to actions for passing off or trade mark infringement.

The relevant provisions concerning trade mark infringement are contained in the Trade Marks Act 1994. Section 10 of the Trade Marks Act 1994 provides that (subject to defences contained in the Act) there will be infringement if, without the proprietor's consent, a person uses, in the course of trade, a sign which is identical with or similar to the trade mark, and is used in relation to goods or services which are identical to those for which the mark is registered; or if the sign is identical and the goods and services are similar. Where, in either case, the goods and services or the sign and the mark being compared are not identical but only similar,

---

1   It is a provision of the draft order referred to at footnote 2 on p 21 that instead of the statutory declaration, a statement may be made in an application to be submitted electronically to the Registrar; but the penalties for making a false statement will be the same as the penalties for making a false declaration.
2   Companies Act 1985, s 30(4).
3   Companies Act 1985, s 31(2).
4   Companies Act 1985, s 31(1).
5   Companies Act 1985, s 30(7).

infringement will occur only if there exists a likelihood of confusion between the mark and the sign. In the case of well-known marks (where the trade mark has a reputation in the UK) there can be trade mark infringement even if neither the goods or services nor the sign in question are identical to those registered, provided they are similar and the use of the sign, without due cause, takes unfair advantage of, or is detrimental to, the distinctive character or the repute of the trade mark. One of the defences provided in the Trade Marks Act 1994 is that the use by a company (or indeed a natural person) of its own name or address does not constitute trade mark infringement.[1]

2.3.9   Passing off

'Passing off' is a tort which is committed where there is damage to a trader's goodwill because another trader is using a name which is the same as or similar to his name. Lord Diplock in *Warnink v Townend*[2] identified five characteristics which had to be present in order for there to be passing off:

> 'My Lords, *Spalding v Gamage*[3] and the later cases make it possible to identify five characteristics which must be present in order to create a valid cause of action for passing off: (1) a misrepresentation (2) made by a trader in the course of trade (3) to prospective customers of his or ultimate consumers of goods or services supplied by him, (4) which is calculated to injure the business or goodwill of another trader (in the sense that this is a reasonably foreseeable consequence) and (5) which causes actual damage to a business or goodwill of the trader by whom the action is brought or (in a *quia timet* action) will probably do so.'

It is now thought that this classic explanation of the tort of passing off was a summary of the position shown in the cases decided before 1980, and the parameters of the tort will move over time. A company name used in the course of trade can be a misrepresentation capable of passing off.[4] Furthermore, the courts will intervene to prevent passing off before it occurs, if the defendant has equipped himself with or intends to equip another with an instrument of fraud. In *Glaxo plc v Glaxowellcome Ltd*,[5] the second and third defendants formed the first defendant company in anticipation of the merger of Glaxo and Wellcome intending to demand that the plaintiffs pay £100,000 for the name Glaxowellcome Ltd. Lightman J held that the defendants had made a dishonest scheme to appropriate the goodwill of the plaintiff and to extort a substantial sum as the price for not damaging the plaintiffs' goodwill. He said (at page 391):

> 'The court will not countenance any such pre-emptive strike of registering companies with names where others have the goodwill in those names and

---

1   Trade Marks Act 1994, s 11(2)(a).
2   (1980) RPC 31 at 93.
3   *A G Spalding & Bros v A W Gamage Ltd* (1915) 32 RPC 273.
4   *Fine Cotton Spinners v Cash* [1907] 2 Ch 184.
5   [1996] FSR 388. See also *Direct Line Group Ltd v Direct Line Estate Agency Ltd* [1997] FSR 374.

the registering party then demanding a price for changing the names. It is an abuse of the system of registration of company names. The right to choose the name with which a company is registered is not given for that purpose.'

2.3.10   Remedies for trade mark infringement or passing off

A court may order the offending company to change its name, and may also grant an injunction to prevent the company doing business under the infringing name. Where the company is already doing business under the name, the operation of the injunction will usually be suspended to allow, the company time to change its name. Damages or an account of profits may also be ordered for trade mark infringement and passing off.

2.4   THE OBJECTS CLAUSE

2.4.1   The function of the objects clause

The objects clause sets out the purposes for which the company is established. In the case of a property management company, the purposes are limited and so the memorandum will contain a fairly simple objects clause.[1] Where the purposes of the company are more complex, the promoters will need to consider carefully what should be included. Before the reforms of company law which started with the UK's entry into the European Community, the doctrine of ultra vires meant that activities which were not within the objects clause of the company could be challenged not only by members of the company but also by the company itself or by the other party to the transaction.[2] This doctrine was reduced in scope by the Companies Act 1985 and effectively abolished[3] by the Companies Act 1989, which inserted a new s 35 into the Companies Act 1985:

> 'The validity of an act done by a company shall not be called into question on the ground of lack of capacity by reason of anything in the company's memorandum.'

However, the objects clause is still an important clause in that it tells members and prospective members why the company exists and what it does. The parameters set by the objects clause should not be so narrow that they hinder the company's activities. In the case of companies limited by guarantee set up to promote particular aims, the promoters often think that they should publicise the explicit purposes of the company. It is a key proposal of the Company Law Review that the requirement to have an objects clause should be abolished. It is likely, however, that at least in the

---

1   For example 'The objects of the company are to manage the freehold or leasehold property known as ...'. See Appendix A1.
2   *Ashbury Railway Carriage and Iron Co Ltd v Riche* (1875) LR 7 HL 653.
3   Except for charities: see **2.4.2**.

case of companies limited by guarantee, a company will be able to continue to define its purposes in an objects clause.

2.4.2 Charitable companies

It is the objects clause that governs whether or not a company is formed for charitable purposes, and so this is the provision of the memorandum at which the Charity Commissioners will look most closely when considering an application for registration as a charity. A brief summary of the meaning of charitable purposes is set out in Chapter 1[1] but readers should refer to specialist texts on charity law or to the Charity Commissioners' publications for a more detailed discussion. The inclusion of one non-charitable object will disqualify the company from registration as a charity, however well the remainder of the objects fit within the accepted definition of charity. Conversely, if the objects of a company are exclusively charitable, then under s 3(7) of the Charities Act 1993, the trustees of the charity have a duty to register the charity with the Charity Commissioners unless it falls within one of the exemptions in s 3(5). Therefore, if the aim is not to create a charity, then a non-charitable object should be included in the memorandum.

The objects clause has a further added significance in the case of companies which are charities. Section 35 of the Companies Act 1985 validates transactions only with a person who either does not know that the company is a charity, or who gives full value for the act in question and who does not know that the act is beyond the capacity of the company as stated in the memorandum. Ultra vires, non-commercial transactions with persons who know that they are dealing with a charity and know that the act is beyond the charity's powers are void, but a person who subsequently acquires property in good faith, without actual knowledge of the ultra vires nature of the earlier transaction, and for full consideration, will nevertheless acquire good title to the property. So, for example, if a person who knows all the circumstances buys property from a charity and does not pay the full market rate, he cannot claim that the transaction was validated by s 35 of the Companies Act 1985, and the sale would be void. However, if in the meantime he had sold the property on at full market value to another person who did not know the details of the previous transaction, the subsequent purchaser's title to the property could not be challenged on this ground.

2.4.3 Insurance companies

An insurance company to which the Insurance Companies Act 1982 applies must not carry on any activities, in the UK or elsewhere, otherwise than in connection with or for the purposes of its insurance business.[2]

---

1   See **1.7.1**.
2   Insurance Companies Act 1982, s 16.

2.4.4   Registered social landlords

A registered social landlord must be established for the purposes of the provision, construction, improvement or management of houses for letting or houses for occupation by its members. Certain additional objects are permitted and these include providing maintenance services and providing advice on the running of housing associations.[1]

2.4.5   Short form objects clauses

The provisions of the Companies Act 1985, inserted by the Companies Act 1989, which permit a company to dispense with the traditional long form objects clause[2] apply equally to companies limited by guarantee. Therefore, where it is desired that the company is to carry on business as a general commercial company, then the objects clause may simply state this fact, and s 3A of the Companies Act 1985 implies that the objects of the company are to carry on any trade or business whatsoever, and the company will have all powers that are incidental or conducive to the carrying on of that object. However, it is unlikely that a company limited by guarantee will be the appropriate form of corporate vehicle for a general commercial company. No non-commercial activities are permitted in the case of a company with the short form objects clause; this would include the making of gifts or charitable donations. Practitioners doubt the usefulness of the s 3A objects clause and the Company Law Review proposes that it should be abolished for new companies.

2.5   THE COMPANY'S POWERS

2.5.1   The function of the statement of powers

The clause of the memorandum which sets out the objects or the next following clause will commonly set out the powers which the company may properly exercise in support of the objects. It is usual for these to be set out at great length; and although judges over the years have expressed disapproval of this practice as it has developed,[3] it may be helpful for the issue to be considered by the promoters of the company. A company will have the power to do anything which can be said to be in support of its objects, but there are several express powers which may be required. An example is the power to set up pension schemes for directors and employees. A company does not, in the absence of an express provision, have the power to give away all of its undertaking, which might be necessary as part of a scheme of reconstruction.[4]

---

1   Housing Act 1996, s 2(2) and (4).
2   Companies Act 1985, s 3A.
3   For example, Lord Wrenbury in *Cotman v Brougham* [1918] AC 514 at 523.
4   *Brady v Brady* (1988) 4 BCC 390, HL.

2.5.2 The effect of acts which are not within the powers of the company

Before the reforms introduced in the Companies Act 1989, an act done by the directors of a company could be challenged on the ordinary principles of agency law relating to the agent's authority: a person dealing with the company could not claim that an act was not authorised by the company (the principal in the agency relationship) if it was within the powers conferred by the memorandum.[1] Section 35A of the Companies Act 1985 now provides that:

> 'In favour of a person dealing in good faith, the power of the board of directors to bind the company, or authorise others to do so, shall be deemed to be free of any limitation under the company's constitution.'

A person is not taken to be in bad faith just because he knows that the act is beyond the powers in the company's constitution.[2] The directors' authority rules are, therefore, now considerably reduced in scope but this does not mean that the clause dealing with the powers of the company is not important. A member of the company may still challenge an act on this basis. The reforms do not affect the liability of directors or any other person by reason of the directors' exceeding their powers,[3] and have a more limited effect in relation to charities.[4]

2.6 DISTRIBUTIONS TO MEMBERS

2.6.1 Charities

In the case of a company that is to be registered as a charity, the Charity Commissioners require the memorandum to contain a provision preventing the distribution of the income and capital profits of the company to its members. On a winding up, any surplus remaining after all the debts of the company have been paid off must be paid to another charity and this restriction should be contained in the memorandum. It is possible to specify another named charity or organisation, but this is not generally advisable as the specified charity may well have ceased to exist, changed its name or amalgamated with another charity by the time the clause comes to be put into effect. It is preferable to specify that the money should be paid over to a charity having similar objects, or having a specified object which is sufficiently broad that there will be no difficulty in applying the money when the time comes (for example, 'the relief of poverty', or even, 'to some charitable object').

---

1   *Rolled Steel Products (Holdings) Ltd v British Steel Corporation* [1985] 3 All ER 52, CA.
2   Companies Act 1985, s 35A(2)(b).
3   Companies Act 1985, s 35A(4) and (5).
4   See Chapter 4.

2.6.2   Other 'not-for-profit' companies

Companies that are not charities may also include this clause in their
memorandum. In particular, it is essential to do so if it is desired to omit the
word 'limited' from the company name under s 30(1)(a) of the Companies
Act 1985.[1] Where a company is set up for purposes that are not charitable,
but which are not primarily for the generation of profit, the inclusion of this
clause makes it clear to members that they do not join the company in order
to make money, but rather to support the philanthropic purposes for which
the company was formed.

These companies, which include trade associations, pressure groups, social
clubs, and quasi-public organisations are collectively called 'not-for-profit'
companies, but this title often causes confusion. Many of these companies
may generate huge profits, particularly trade associations of which the
members themselves are successful commercial companies. Neither the
label 'not-for-profit', nor the inclusion of the no-distribution clause, means
that the company is not intended to generate profit. Rather it means that
any profit it does generate is not distributed as a dividend, but must be
applied for the purposes of the company.

There are two disadvantages of a not-for-profit company accumulating
surpluses. First, unless the company is a charity or a scientific research
association,[2] any profits which have not been spent at the end of the year are
subject to corporation tax. Secondly, the regular accumulation of surpluses
may lead the members of the company to conclude that the directors are not
properly managing the company, particularly where the bulk of the funds of
the company are provided by the members by way of membership fees or
otherwise.

2.6.3   Benefits that are not distributions

Not-for-profit companies sometimes provide to their members benefits in
kind. An example is a trade association which is set up by a group of
companies in order to share information, or provide a centralised service.
Such a company may provide information or facilities on a fully-
commercial or a subsidised basis to its members or to their employees or
customers. This raises the question of whether the company can be said to
be contravening the no-distribution clause, since the benefits provided
could be said to be a form of distribution. It is submitted that this is a false
argument. The common form of 'no distribution' clause will not prohibit
any benefits being conferred on members, but will prohibit distributions 'by
way of profit'. Profit is the money a company has left after paying all its
expenses. If the benefits to the members are properly incurred expenses
within the objects of the company, then there is no reason why the company
should not benefit the members in this way. Put another way, if the reason

1   See **2.3.7**.
2   See **1.7.7**.

the company was set up was to benefit the members then the existence of the 'no distribution' clause does not detract from this aim. Everything will turn on the interpretation of the objects clause, and the scope of the company's powers.

2.6.4   Benefits to charity members

The exception to the principle set out at **2.6.3** occurs where the company is a charity, and the members who receive benefits are also charity trustees. The general principle is that charity trustees are expected to act gratuitously.[1] The memorandum may permit them to receive benefits, but usually this is to allow a professional trustee such as a solicitor or an accountant to charge to the charity his professional fees. A clause permitting a trustee to be reimbursed his expenses is also permissible. Exceptionally, the Charity Commissioners will approve the inclusion in the memorandum of a clause which permits a paid managing director to serve as trustee, where this can be demonstrated to be in the best interests of the charity. Equally there may be exceptional circumstances where, in order to attract trustees of a sufficient degree of experience, the charity can justify conferring some benefit upon them, but this will need to be discussed in detail with the Charity Commissioners.

In the absence of a concession from the Charity Commissioners, however, member-trustees must not receive any benefits, whether in cash or in kind, from the company. Examples are accommodation provided at less than a full market rent, the use of other facilities of the charity (such as its office facilities) without a proper charge, and the payment of interest on a loan provided to the charity at a rate of interest higher than the prevailing bank rate. Even an annual dinner or other celebration for the members may contravene the 'no benefit' rule if the amount spent on it is disproportionate to the income of the charity and it cannot be justified as a fund-raising or profile-raising occasion.

2.6.5   Benefits to members of registered social landlords

A registered social landlord may not make a gift or pay a sum by way of dividend or bonus to a person who is or has been (or a member of whose family is or has been) a member of it, or is a company of which the person or family member is a director, except certain interest payments on capital loans to the company, or payments due under tenancy agreements.[2]

---

1   *Re Barber* (1886) 34 ChD 77.
2   Housing Act 1996, s 7, and Sch 1, para 1.

2.7 THE GUARANTEE

Section 2(4) of the Companies Act 1985 provides:

> 'The memorandum of a company limited by guarantee must also state that each member undertakes to contribute to the assets of the company if it should be wound up while he is a member, or within one year after he ceases to be a member, for payment of the debts and liabilities of the company contracted before he ceases to be a member, and of the costs, charges and expenses of winding up, and for adjustment of the rights of the contributories among themselves, such amount as may be required, not exceeding a specified amount.'

This represents the guarantee given by members, ie the limit of their liability. The specified amount can be a nominal amount, usually £1 or £10, and is only payable if on winding up the company there are insufficient funds to satisfy all the company's creditors. It is a debt due from the member to the company.[1] It is not to be confused with any membership fee or subscription required by the articles or rules, as a condition of joining the company or of maintaining membership while the company carries on business. The guarantee fund can be regarded as in the nature of reserve capital and cannot be charged by the company.[2] If any working capital is required it is usually contributed as loans to the company.

It would be possible for there to be different levels of the guarantee required of different classes of members, and for the rights to participate in any distribution of surplus on a winding-up to be linked to the amount of the guarantee of each member. This might be appropriate in a case where a club is incorporated, or where there are founder members of the company who contribute much more than the new members in terms of funding the company or in terms of the effort contributed to its establishment.

One of the proposals of the Company Law Review is for the guarantee to take a different form, perhaps in the statement of the first directors and secretary of the company which is submitted to Companies House on incorporation.

---

1   Companies Act 1985, s 14(2).
2   Compare s 120 of the Companies Act 1985, and *Re Irish Club* [1906] WN 127, *Re Pyle Works* (1890) 44 ChD 534, 59 LJ Ch 489, CA.

2.8 ALTERATION OF THE MEMORANDUM

2.8.1 When is alteration permitted?

The memorandum may be altered only to the extent set out in the Companies Act 1985.[1] The Act permits the alteration of the name,[2] the objects clause,[3] and any condition (other than a provision which confers rights upon a particular class or classes of member) which could have lawfully been contained in the articles, unless the memorandum itself prohibits such alteration.[4] In the case of changes other than a change of name, any member of the company has the right to petition the court in order to have the alteration revoked.

2.8.2 Alteration of the objects clause

A company may alter its objects clause by means of a special resolution.[5] A copy of the resolution and of the memorandum as altered must be filed at Companies House within 15 days after the change.[6] The former restrictions on the scope of permissible alterations were removed by the Companies Act 1989. However, if the company is a charity then it may not alter its objects clause in any respect without first obtaining the consent of the Charity Commissioners.[7] A copy of the letter of consent must be filed at Companies House when the special resolution is filed.[8] This is so that the Charity Commissioners may ensure that a company may not obtain the benefits of registration as a charity and then change its objects so as to cease to be charitable.

A company which is an insurance company within the meaning of the Insurance Companies Act 1982 may not conduct activities which are not insurance business, otherwise than in connection with or for the purpose of its insurance business.[9] A company registered as a social landlord may not change its objects clause without the consent of the Housing Corporation.[10]

2.8.3 Change of name

A company limited by guarantee may change its name by passing a special resolution.[11] A copy of the resolution must be filed at Companies House

---

1 Companies Act 1985, s 2(7).
2 See **2.8.3**.
3 See **2.8.2**.
4 Companies Act 1985, s 17.
5 Companies Act 1985, s 4.
6 Companies Act 1985, s 380(1).
7 Charities Act 1983, s 64(2).
8 Charities Act 1993, s 64(3).
9 Insurance Companies Act 1982, s 16.
10 Housing Act 1996, s 7 and Sch 1, para 11.
11 Companies Act 1985, s 28.

within 15 days after the date of the resolution.[1] There is a fee for the registration of a change of name, currently £10 (or £100 in the case of a change of name to be effected on the day of presentation). Companies House will refuse to register a change of name if the new name does not comply with the rules set out at **2.3.3** and **2.3.4**. A registered social landlord must notify the Housing Corporation of a change of name.[2]

2.8.4   Change to exclude the word 'limited'

A company limited by guarantee may change its name so that it becomes exempt from the requirement to include the word 'limited' or 'cyfyngedig' at the end of its name, provided that after the change the name satisfies the requirements of s 30 of the Companies Act 1985.[3] It may also be necessary to change the objects clause and the distribution clause in order to bring a company within the section.

2.8.5   Change of name by a charity

A registered charity may also change its name by the same procedure, but the name will not be recognised by the Charity Commission unless the name complies with the rules set out at **2.3.6**. It is sensible to check that the proposed name complies with those rules before the name change is proposed to the members and the special resolution is passed, which in practice means before any notice of general meeting or written resolution is sent out. Otherwise, if the name is refused by the Charity Commission, the company would be obliged to go through the same procedure again. If the change of name is designed to reflect the changed circumstances of the charity, the trustees should consider whether or not any changes to the objects of the charity are necessary.

2.8.6   Change of registered office

The memorandum must state that the registered office of a company is to be situated in England and Wales; in Wales; or in Scotland.[4] A change to the location of a company's registered office within the country of its incorporation does not require the memorandum to be altered. This is a matter for the directors of the company who may alter the location of the registered office by a board resolution.[5] The change does not take effect until form 287 is filed at Companies House, although the previous address remains effective for the purpose of serving documents on the company for a period of 14 days after registration.[6] A registered social landlord is

---

1   Companies Act 1985, s 380(1).
2   Housing Act 1996, Sch 1, para 11.
3   See **2.3.7**.
4   Companies Act 1985, s 2(1)(b).
5   Companies Act 1985, s 287(3) states that this may be done by the company, therefore, unless the articles reserve this power to the members, it is within the general powers of management of the directors.
6   Companies Act 1985, s 287(4).

required to notify the Housing Corporation of changes to its registered office address.[1]

However, with one exception, a company may not change the country of its registered office as stated in the memorandum, as the Companies Act 1985 provides no mechanism for this. The exception is that a company incorporated in England and Wales, whose registered office is in Wales, may alter its memorandum by special resolution so that the reference to England is removed.[2] There is no power to reverse this change. A company whose registered office is in Wales may use the word 'cyfyngedig' at the end of its name but not elsewhere in its name, and if the location of the registered office is changed the name may also be changed to substitute the word 'cyfyngedig' for the word 'limited'.[3]

2.8.7 Change to the powers and distribution clauses

As set out at **2.8.1**, most of the other conditions contained in the memorandum may be altered by special resolution. A company limited by guarantee may change a clause which prohibits the distribution of income to members, so as to permit a dividend; and it may change the clause which restricts the distribution of assets on a winding up, unless in either case the memorandum prohibits such a change. However, changes of this sort would disqualify the company from the exemption in s 30 of the Companies Act 1985,[4] and would, in the case of a charity, require the prior written consent of the Charity Commissioners in order to be effective.[5] The copy resolution and revised memorandum required to be delivered to the registrar of companies must be accompanied by a copy of the Charity Commissioners' consent.[6] Similarly, in the case of a registered social landlord, any alteration to the memorandum of the company is not valid without the consent of the Housing Corporation and a copy of the consent must be sent to Companies House.[7]

However, s 17 of the Companies Act 1985 refers only to the alteration of conditions contained in the memorandum. It does not specifically authorise the addition of new clauses into the memorandum, for example when a company whose memorandum is silent on the question of distribution of profits wishes to become a not-for-profit company. Prior to the enactment of the predecessor of s 17 in the Companies Act 1948, it was held that a company could not alter or add to its memorandum unless the memorandum authorised alterations or additions to itself, or referred to a procedure in the articles by which provisions could be altered or added.[8] It

---

1   Housing Act 1996, Sch 1, para 11.
2   Companies Act 1985, s 2(2).
3   Companies Act 1985, s 2(5).
4   See **2.3.7**.
5   Charities Act 1993, s 64(2)(b).
6   Charities Act 1993, s 64(3).
7   Housing Act 1996, s 7 and Sch 1, para 11.
8   *Ashbury v Watson* (1885) 30 ChD 376, CA.

is thought that this principle continues to apply to amendments which are outside the scope of s 17. Unless there is authority in the memorandum for the addition of new clauses, therefore, they should be inserted into the articles. When a clause in the memorandum is simply deleted (for example, a power conferred upon the company to make distributions in kind) the remaining clauses should not be renumbered, but a note should be inserted at the relevant place to the effect that a clause has been deleted by a special resolution passed on a stated date.

2.8.8 Alteration of the guarantee

A company limited by guarantee may not alter the clause which sets out the guarantee[1] as there is no provision in the Companies Act 1985 for this change: the clause must be in the memorandum and so even s 17 of the Companies Act 1985 will not help. Equally, it is not possible to 'convert' a company limited by guarantee into a company limited by shares, either by re-registration or by providing for shares in the memorandum or articles.[2] It is, however, possible for a company limited by guarantee to re-register as an unlimited company, but this requires a particular procedure to be followed which includes obtaining the consent of all the members.[3] The procedure cannot be reversed, ie a company that has previously re-registered as unlimited may not be re-registered as limited.[4]

2.8.9 Entrenchment

Occasionally, when a company limited by guarantee is being set up, the promoters may wish to legislate against any future alteration of certain provisions of the memorandum. In the case of a private company limited by shares, it is common for there to be a shareholders' agreement supplementing the statutory constitution, but an equivalent in a company limited by guarantee would be unusual, as the membership of a company limited by guarantee is likely to be more fluid. Therefore, the question of entrenching provisions of the constitution may be raised.

There are levels of entrenchment. One occurs where the memorandum provides that a particular provision may not be altered except by a resolution of the company in general meeting passed by a specified majority. The Companies Act 1985 provides for a special resolution to be passed by a majority of at least three-quarters of the members voting for or against the resolution at a properly convened general meeting of the company.[5] Any provision in the constitution which provides for a lower majority is of no effect, but the Companies Act 1985 does not prevent the inclusion of a provision requiring a higher majority. If a higher majority is

---

1   *Hennessy v National Agricultural and Industrial Development Association* [1947] IR 159.
2   See Companies Act 1985, s 15.
3   Companies Act 1985, s 49.
4   Companies Act 1985, ss 43(1) and 51(2).
5   Companies Act 1985, s 378.

specified, the resolution remains a special resolution for the purposes of the Act.

Particularly where a company has replaced the usual 'one member, one vote' provision with weighted voting rights, there may be a fear that it would be too easy for a group of members to collude to alter the constitution: for example, to change the objects clause. It is sometimes thought desirable to entrench further and to provide in the memorandum that the provision may not be changed at all.

Care should be taken with drafting an entrenchment provision, either in the original memorandum or in the wording of a special resolution to insert it, as the entrenching provision is one which could lawfully have been contained in the articles and so s 17 of the Companies Act 1985 will allow it to be changed. The clause which states that a particular majority must be in favour of a proposed change, or that no change can be made, can itself be changed or removed altogether unless it is expressly set out in the memorandum and the clause itself states that no alteration may be made to it. A clause set out separately ('no alteration may be made to clause x') will not have the effect of entrenching clause x, because clause x could lawfully have been in the articles.[1] In order to entrench via a separate clause, the wording would need to be: 'no alteration may be made to clause x or to this clause'.

However, it is rarely advisable for a company limited by guarantee to entrench provisions of its memorandum. The circumstances of the company may change; its membership may change over time; and the market in which it operates may also change. If a clause (other than a class rights clause)[2] is fully entrenched, the only options for overcoming it would be either to wind up the company, form a replacement, and transfer the assets to the new company, or to propose a scheme of arrangement under s 425 of the Companies Act 1985, which requires the court's approval.[3]

2.9 THE ARTICLES OF ASSOCIATION

2.9.1 Function and form

The articles of association of a company contain the detailed administrative rules of the company. The memorandum is concerned with the relationship with the outside world but the articles govern the relationship of the members between themselves, their relationship with the board of directors and with the company itself.

---

1   Although Neuberger J in *Re RAC Motoring Services Ltd* [2000] 1 BCLC 307 expressed the view that a court might read such provisions together to give effect to the intended purpose of the clause.
2   See **3.11** on class rights.
3   See **6.8**.

If there is any conflict between the articles or a resolution to alter them and the memorandum then the terms of the memorandum will prevail;[1] and the articles cannot be used to fill gaps in the memorandum to the extent that the contents of the memorandum are dictated by law. However, the articles can be used as an aid to interpretation of the memorandum where there is ambiguity or incompleteness in the memorandum.[2] The articles are generally to be construed as a commercial document although the court has no power to rectify the articles.[3] The articles must not contain anything which is illegal or contrary to public policy; although the effect of including such a provision would presumably be to render the particular article void rather than to invalidate the whole document, unless deletion of the offending article would render the remaining articles meaningless.

2.9.2 Table C

A company limited by guarantee must register articles.[4] Unlike the case of a company limited by shares, Table A[5] will not apply if the company does not register any articles. Section 8 of the Companies Act 1985 provides that the articles of association 'shall be ... in accordance with Table C ...'. Table C uses Table A as its basis, amending the articles individually to remove references to shares and shareholders. Note that if Table A is incorporated by reference into a set of articles, the company is governed by the version of Table A which was current when the articles were adopted.

It may be confusing if the articles of a company limited by guarantee refer to another set of articles, particularly where those other articles were designed for a company limited by shares. Where the articles are likely to be referred to frequently, or are likely to be controversial among the members, it may be preferable to adopt complete and self-contained articles. There is no need, as is the usual practice in a company limited by shares, to include in the bespoke articles a provision excluding Table A in its entirety.[6] However, if bespoke articles are adopted, care should be taken to include provisions dealing with the admission and removal of members, and if desired, to confer upon members the power to appoint proxies, as the Companies Act 1985 implies this only in the case of a company limited by shares.[7]

---

1   *Ashbury v Watson* (1885) 30 ChD 376, CA.
2   *Angostura Bitters (Dr JGB Siegert & Sons) Ltd v Kerr* [1933] AC 550 at 554, PC.
3   *Scott v Frank F Scott (London) Ltd* [1940] Ch 794, CA.
4   Companies Act 1985, s 7(1).
5   Companies (Tables A to F) Regulations 1985, SI 1985/805 as amended by SI 1985/1052.
6   Companies Act 1985, s 8(2).
7   Companies Act 1985, s 372(2)(a).

2.10 THE EFFECT OF THE ARTICLES AS A CONTRACT

Very early companies were formed by each member executing a deed which formed a contract between them; and when a new member joined a new deed would have to be executed, novating the contract. The modern equivalent of this principle is contained in s 14(1) of the Companies Act 1985:

> 'Subject to the provisions of this Act, the memorandum and articles, when registered, bind the company and its members to the same extent as if they respectively had been signed and sealed by each member, and contained covenants on the part of each member to observe all the provisions of the memorandum and of the articles.'

The articles are, therefore, a form of contract, although the principles of the law of contract cannot be applied to them without modification. The articles bind the members only as members, and not (for example) in their capacity as directors.[1] The articles also bind the company and the company can sue and be sued on the contract formed by the articles. The articles, although they are contained in a constitutional document available on the public register, do not bind or confer any rights on people who are not members of the company, such as its employees; although they may be incorporated by reference into the terms of an extrinsic contract. Enforcement of the rights conferred by the articles is also different in nature from the enforcement of normal contractual rights: unless the rights are classified as 'personal rights' of members, or there is a non-ratifiable breach of the articles by the company, there are restrictions on enforcement of the rights by an individual member.[2]

2.11 ALTERATION OF THE ARTICLES

2.11.1 Restricting the power to alter the articles

Section 9 of the Companies Act 1985 confers the power to alter the articles, subject to the provisions of the memorandum and the Act. The articles, unlike the memorandum, cannot be entrenched to such a degree that alteration is not possible, as the company cannot deprive itself of the statutory power.[3] However, although the position is not certain, it may be possible as a result of the decision in *Bushell v Faith*[4] to restrict the exercise of the power to alter, by giving members weighted voting rights on

---

1   *Hickman v Kent or Romney Marsh Sheep-Breeders' Association* [1915] 1 Ch 881.
2   See **4.5.9**.
3   *Allen v Gold Reefs of West Africa Ltd* [1900] 1 Ch 656, CA.
4   [1970] AC 1099, [1970] 2 WLR 272, [1970] 1 All ER 53, HL. The case concerned a company limited by shares which was owner-managed. However, the ratio of the case is not confined to such companies.

particular types of resolution. This might be useful, for example, where the founders of a not-for-profit company wish to ensure that future members will not alter the ethos of the company, but do not wish to go as far as entrenching the provisions by including them in an unalterable provision in the memorandum.[1]

2.11.2   Weighted voting rights: *Bushell v Faith*

The question for the court in *Bushell v Faith* was whether weighted voting rights could be given in the articles to enable a member to prevent his removal from the office of director under what is now s 303 of the Companies Act 1985. The decision is, therefore, strictly speaking confined to weighted voting rights in that context. Although reference was made in the case to the right of the company to 'issue shares with such rights as the company may by ordinary resolution determine', it is arguable that this was not necessary for the decision and that, therefore the case should apply with equal force to a company limited by guarantee. The outstanding question is whether the principle will apply to weighted voting rights on a resolution to alter the articles. These rights were included in the articles of the company in the case of *Re National Farmers' Union Development Trust Ltd*,[2] but their validity was not in issue in the case. It has been argued that this would contravene the principle that the articles cannot be entrenched. However, the majority of the House of Lords in *Bushell v Faith* held that the mischief addressed by s 303 was not the use of weighted voting rights but the use of clauses which require more than a simple majority in order to remove a director. It could be argued that the same reasoning should apply to s 9 of the Companies Act 1985, which states that a company may alter its articles by special resolution, but does not state that this applies 'notwithstanding anything in the articles' (as does s 303). In other words, it is possible that provided the articles do require alterations to be made by a greater majority than that specified by the Act, weighted voting rights may validly be included in the articles to prevent specific alterations to the articles.

Bushell v Faith was referred to in the judgment of the House of Lords in *Russell v Northern Bank Development Corporation Ltd*[3] which decided that any provision in a company's articles which restricts the company's statutory power to alter its articles is invalid; but the court did not take the opportunity to explain or to restrict the scope of *Bushell v Faith*. The effectiveness of weighted voting rights in the articles, therefore, remains uncertain.

The position is more certain in the case of weighted voting rights contained in the memorandum, since s 9 specifically states that the power to alter is subject to the Companies Act 1985 and to any conditions contained in the company's memorandum. Care should, however, be taken to ensure that

---

1   See **2.8.9**.
2   [1972] 1 WLR 1548, [1973] 1 All ER 135.
3   [1992] 1 WLR 588, HL.

the weighted voting rights apply equally to resolutions to alter the clause in the memorandum itself.[1]

2.11.3 Restrictions on the scope of alterations

An alteration to the articles must not conflict with the terms of the memorandum, or with an order of the court.[2] Furthermore, the alteration must not require an existing member to increase his contribution to the capital of the company (for example, under the guarantee clause) or otherwise to pay money to the company, without that member's consent.[3] An alteration may also be a breach of a contract with a third party: for example, a director's service contract may incorporate provisions of the articles by reference; a director may be able to claim damages if the alteration causes him to suffer loss but he cannot prevent or overturn the alteration.

The power to alter must be exercised in good faith in the interests of the company as a whole.[4] However, this does not prevent a member from voting in his own interests, unless, perhaps, there are equitable considerations which make it unjust for a member to exercise his vote in a particular way.[5] The courts have had some difficulty reconciling these ideas in the case of companies limited by shares.[6] However, since the introduction of the members' remedy under s 459 of the Companies Act 1985 the court is generally reluctant to overturn the vote of the majority except where there is unfairly prejudicial conduct within the meaning of s 459.[7]

2.11.4 Charities

In the case of a company which is a charity, there is a restriction on the scope of s 9. An alteration to any provision in the articles 'which is a provision directing or restricting the manner in which the property of the company may be used or applied', is ineffective unless it has the prior written consent of the Charity Commissioners.[8] The copy special resolution filed at Companies House must be accompanied by a copy of the Charity Commissioners' consent.

---

1   See **2.8.1** and Appendix A.
2   For example, an order made under s 461 of the Companies Act 1985.
3   Companies Act 1985, s 16.
4   *Greenhalgh v Arderne Cinemas Ltd* [1951] Ch 286, CA.
5   *Clemens v Clemens Bros Ltd* [1976] 2 All ER 268.
6   See for example *Allen v Gold Reefs of West Africa* [1900] 1Ch 656 and *Sidebottom v Kershaw, Leese & Co* [1920] 1 Ch 154, CA.
7   See **4.5.9**.
8   Charities Act 1993, s 64.

2.12   THE CONTENT OF THE ARTICLES

2.12.1   Changes in membership and the conduct of meetings

The articles will contain detailed provisions relating to the admission and removal of members and the conduct of meetings of the company.[1] These matters are discussed in Chapters 3 and 5 respectively.

2.12.2   Officers of the company

The directors of a company limited by guarantee may be given some other name in the articles, for example: in the case of a charity, 'Trustees'; in the case of a 'not-for-profit' company, 'Members of the Council of Management', or 'Governors'. However, in this book the term 'directors' is used. The name given to the directors in the articles has no effect on the extent of their liability but the directors may also have duties imposed by other sets of laws which apply, for example as charity trustees or as directors of an insurance company.

A company limited by guarantee must have a company secretary. The duties of the company secretary are the keeping of the company's registers such as the register of members and the register of charges, the administration of the meetings of the members and of the board, and the taking of minutes at meetings. The power of appointment is normally given to the board of directors and the board may also remove a secretary appointed by them, subject of course to the terms of employment in the case of a person employed specifically to take that office. There is no equivalent of s 303 of the Companies Act 1985 in the case of the secretary. However, the company secretary is in a fiduciary position like a director and may not make a secret profit from his position.[2] As an officer of the company, the secretary may be made liable for default in compliance with provisions of the Companies Act 1985, particularly those relating to the filing of returns at Companies House.[3]

The articles may also mention other officers such as a President and a Treasurer. There are no provisions of the Act which attach specifically to these offices, and the company is free to make provision in the articles as necessary. The articles should, however, say whether a particular officer is required also to be a director of the company, and the principles set out above relating to the responsibility of the board apply equally here.

Some companies limited by guarantee, particularly those which are charities, may wish to appoint patrons. These are usually figures who are

---

1   Note in particular that the articles of a company limited by guarantee must include an express power to appoint proxies if it is desired that a member of the company should be able to appoint someone to exercise his vote in his absence: see **5.4.7**.

2   See Chapter 4.

3   Companies House publishes useful guidelines which describe the role of the directors and secretary: see www.companieshouse.gov.uk.

well-known nationally or locally who give their support (financial or otherwise) to the organisation. These people are not officers of the company and their appointment does not need to be authorised by the articles. Care should be taken, however, if their names are shown on the company notepaper as it should be easy to distinguish the patrons' names from those of the directors.

Provisions of the articles relating to directors are discussed in detail in Chapter 4.

2.12.3   Minutes and other records

The articles often provide that minutes must be kept of general meetings and board meetings. In any event, the provisions relating to minutes are set out in ss 382 to 383 of the Companies Act 1985.[1] It may be helpful to put a reminder in the articles that minutes should be kept of all meetings in accordance with the Act. The same could be said of the obligation to keep books of account although it is inadvisable to do any more than refer to the Act, as the company will not be able to take advantage of any relaxations of the accounting or auditing rules if its articles make provision for the accounts to be prepared in a particular form.

2.12.4   The company seal

Section 36A of the Companies Act 1985 provides for a choice (in the case of companies in England and Wales) as to whether or not to have a company seal. A company may execute documents by affixing the seal, but the company is not obliged to have a seal. Whether or not it has a seal, a document signed by a director and the secretary or a second director is effective as if the seal had been affixed. Section 36B provides that a company is not obliged to have a seal 'notwithstanding the provisions of any enactment'. Table A is in an 'enactment' because the section states that 'enactment' includes a statutory instrument. Table A, reg 101 implies that the company has a seal. In the case of a company limited by shares there is an argument that if the company does not file articles and relies on Table A it is no longer obliged to have a seal. However, a company limited by guarantee must file articles and although some companies do file articles which adopt certain parts of Table A it could be argued that reg 101 is no longer, in this instance, merely an 'enactment' but has been fully incorporated into the articles of the company. Therefore, in the case of a company limited by guarantee, it is safer to assume that any reference in the articles to a seal is a mandatory provision.

2.12.5   Notices

The articles should contain a clause which sets out how notices may be served and when a notice served by an authorised method is to be taken to have arrived at its destination. The Companies Act 1985 provides that if the

---

1   See Chapter 5.

articles do not contain this provision then notices are to be served in the manner set out in Table A,[1] but this means having two sources of reference, and in any event, the company may wish to adopt methods of serving notices which are not permitted by Table A. Furthermore, the provisions of Table A refer to the holders of shares, and in most companies limited by guarantee there will be no shareholders.

Table A[2] provides that notices to members must be in writing, and:

> 'the company may give any notice to a member either personally or by sending it by post in a prepaid envelope addressed to the member at his registered address or by leaving it at that address...'
>
> 'Proof that an envelope containing a notice was properly addressed, prepaid and posted shall be conclusive evidence that the notice was given. A notice shall be deemed to be given at the expiration of 48 hours after the envelope containing it was posted'.

According to Table A:

> 'a member whose registered address is not within the United Kingdom and who gives to the company an address within the United Kingdom at which notices may be given to him shall be entitled to have notices given to him at that address, but otherwise no such member shall be entitled to receive any notice from the company'.

If there is to be a significant international membership, the articles should provide for notices to be required to be served to international addresses, but allowance for the additional time taken for postal deliveries should be included, or perhaps service by international courier should be made mandatory.

Regulation 113 of Table A provides:

> 'a member present, either in person or by proxy, at any meeting of the company or of the holders of any class of shares in the company shall be deemed to have received notice of the meeting and, where requisite, of the purposes for which it was called'.

It should be noted that this applies only to the class meetings of shareholders and not also to class meetings of members. It also assumes that a member has the right to appoint a proxy, which is not automatically the case in a company limited by guarantee. This serves as an illustration of how the provisions of Table A, which were specifically drafted as regulations for the management of a company limited by shares, are not appropriate for use by a company limited by guarantee.

The articles may prescribe any method of service but if there is a method set out in the articles it is to be regarded as mandatory. Service by any other method will invalidate the meeting except that if a person whose notice was

---

1   Companies Act 1985, s 370(2) and Companies (Tables A to F) Regulations 1985, SI 1985/805 as amended by SI 1985/1052.

2   The provisions of Table A relating to notices are contained in regs 111 to 116.

not validly served nevertheless attends the meeting, he is deemed to have waived his right to complain about improper service. Traditionally notices have been permitted to be served by post, by hand delivery to an address, or by handing them to members personally. The articles may also authorise service of notices by fax or by e-mail but it is sensible to require this to be by prior arrangement with the recipient: in other words, only members who have given the company a fax number or e-mail address may be served with notice in this manner. In addition, the articles should require evidence of delivery as part of the conditions for the service of a valid notice. In the case of service by fax, the articles should require the sender to receive a clear transmission report from its fax machine, indicating transmission of all the pages to the correct number. In the case of e-mail service of notices, a return receipt e-mail should be required. In each case these receipts should be kept, preferably in printed form. The articles may provide for notices sent by these methods to be deemed to have been served instantaneously.[1]

If a member is situated in enemy territory or is otherwise regarded by the law as an enemy, the law suspends the right of that member to receive notices and accordingly, the requirement of service on every member is adjusted while the enemy status subsists.[2]

2.12.6 Indemnity for officers or auditors

Section 310 of the Companies Act 1985 provides that any provision in the articles or any external contract is void if it exempts an officer or auditor from liability which would otherwise attach to him in relation to any negligence, default, breach of duty or breach of trust in relation to the company. The same rule applies to any indemnity covering the same liabilities, in other words a right to claim reimbursement of damages paid to third parties in respect of those liabilities. The company may insure against these liabilities and may offer an indemnity against liability incurred in defending any civil or criminal proceedings in which judgment is given in the officer's favour or in which he is acquitted, or in any case under s 727 of the Companies Act 1985 in which relief is granted for honest and reasonable conduct. Regulation 118 of Table A gives an indemnity 'subject to the Act' which is the safest approach, since an article in this form cannot be void.

In older companies, the provision will often be found in the memorandum as well as in the articles. The intention behind this may have been to entrench the provisions since what is now s 17 of the Companies Act 1985 was only introduced in the Companies Act 1948, and before that Act a specific authorisation in the memorandum was needed to alter the optional provisions of the memorandum.

---

1   See Appendix A.
2   *Re Anglo-International Bank* [1943] Ch 233.

2.12.7   Rules or by-laws

One feature of the articles of a company limited by guarantee that is rarely seen in the case of a company limited by shares is the inclusion of the power to make rules or by-laws. This power is usually given to the board of directors of the company rather than to the membership. The advantage of doing this is that it allows flexibility, which is not a feature of provisions set out in full in the articles themselves. The board of directors may alter the rules (in accordance with any procedure which may be set out in the articles) as the need arises, whereas the articles may only be altered by a resolution of the members of the company being a special resolution voted upon at a meeting or a written resolution passed by all the members.

However, where the members of the company regard their constitutional role as particularly important, or where the election of directors is a contentious subject, it may not be a good idea from the point of view of maintaining good relations with the members to give the board absolute control over the content of the rules. The articles may provide for some form of consultation exercise to be undertaken. This might be appropriate where the company has a small membership and the rules are to be introduced at a time when the membership is rapidly expanding.

Rules are not registered at Companies House and so are not public documents.[1] However, a prospective member should be referred to the rules in the application form for membership[2] or sent copies before becoming a member. The reason is that the terms of the articles are deemed by s 14 of the Companies Act 1985 to bind every member as if that member had signed them as a contract. The fact of membership therefore automatically incorporates the terms of the articles into the contract; but the same cannot with certainty be said to be true of the rules. It would be open to a court to decide that the rules were incorporated by means of the reference in the articles; but equally a court might decide, on ordinary contractual principles, that the member had not had a reasonable opportunity to inspect the rules before becoming bound to the (statutory) contract; and so the safest course is to draw them to the member's attention at the point at which the application is made.

The articles may leave the list of matters to be the subject of rules to the directors' discretion, or they may provide a closed list; but the best approach is to say that the board may make rules governing any aspect of the company's administration, but set out a non-exhaustive list of subjects. This gives some reassurance to the members of the company that the directors are not being given a completely free rein but maintains the element of flexibility, which is the chief advantage of establishing rules rather than drafting articles.

---

1   Although see below on rules that create class rights.
2   See Appendix C.

Typical matters for rules are:

(1) admission and removal of members;
(2) provisions relating to classes of members;
(3) membership fees and subscriptions;
(4) procedures for meetings of the board and committees;
(5) the use by members of the company's facilities; and
(6) other entitlements of members (eg to newsletters or admission discounts).

The rules need not be drafted in any particular format, although in the interests of clarity it is useful to give each rule a title or a number and to number each separate provision of each rule, as an aid to cross-referencing.

In the articles themselves, it is also useful to state that in the event of any inconsistency between the rules and the memorandum or articles, the terms of the latter will prevail.

2.12.8 Class rights

If the rules of the company create class rights,[1] the company must file at Companies House details of the class rights using form 129. Classes of members may be created which merely have different labels, different qualification criteria and perhaps a different membership fee. These are not class rights; but if the different classes have rights such as weighted voting rights or the right to appoint a different number of directors, these will be categorised as class rights. An amendment to the rules which merely changes the qualifying conditions for membership does not have the effect of transferring members from one class to another.[2]

2.13 OTHER AGREEMENTS OUTSIDE THE ARTICLES

Where there are any rules that are to be made binding on non-members, or on members but not in that capacity, the obligations should be imposed by means of a contract outside the articles. An example of rules which are to bind members but not in their capacity as members might be rules governing the use of the company's premises by members and non-members. Another example is the case of the trade association which provides services to its members or vice versa. If payment is due from a member, it is easier to enforce this as a pure contractual debt. Finally, there may be a need to form a contract with a director: the articles do not bind except in the capacity of member, and so employment contracts, loans, consultancy services and so on should be dealt with outside the articles.

---

1 See **3.11**.
2 *Fletcher and Another v Royal Automobile Club Ltd* (unreported) 3 February 2000, CA.

In each case, the company cannot rely on the statutory mechanism for incorporating the terms of the articles, and should ensure that a binding contract is made which incorporates all the relevant terms. Preferably the contract should be in writing, should name both parties, should contain mutual obligations or payment being made in exchange for goods and services, should deal with duration and termination, and should allocate the risks and liabilities between the parties. Care should be taken when the company is to enter into a contract with a trust, partnership, club or sole trader, to ensure that if there is any dispute, the company can identify who is the legal entity that has entered into the contract, and that the contract has been signed by the correct number of individuals.

In addition, the articles may be interpreted as a term of an extrinsic contract into which they are incorporated by reference. The question then arises as to the effect of alterations of the articles which affect the contract in question. Probably the answer is that if the contract incorporates the article as an article then the power to alter is also impliedly incorporated.[1]

---

1   Most of the cases concern the service contracts of directors see *Read v Astoria Garage (Streatham) Ltd* [1952] Ch 637, CA; *Shindler v Northern Raincoat Co Ltd* [1960] 2 All ER 239; *Southern Foundries (1926) Ltd v Shirlaw* [1940] AC 701.

Chapter 3

MEMBERSHIP

3.1 WHO ARE THE MEMBERS OF A COMPANY LIMITED BY GUARANTEE?

3.1.1 The role of the members

Even if the members of the company do not have rights of ownership in the company, because the profits of the company cannot be distributed to them, and the surplus on a winding up is to be paid to another organisation rather than to the members, they do have an important constitutional role. They do not normally have day-to-day control over the company's affairs, but they are able to control changes in the constitution[1] and other fundamental decisions relating to the company.[2] In particular, the members' right to remove a director by an ordinary resolution of which special notice has been given cannot be taken away from them.[3] The liability of the members is limited to the amount they have agreed to contribute, set out in the guarantee clause of the memorandum.[4] This liability cannot be extended unless they have received an unlawful dividend.[5]

3.1.2 The subscribers

As in the case of a company limited by shares, the first members of a company limited by guarantee are the persons who have signed their names at the end of ('subscribed to') the memorandum and articles submitted to Companies House for incorporation. Section 22(1) of the Companies Act 1985 provides that the subscribers to the memorandum are deemed to have agreed to become members of the company's incorporation. Once the registrar of companies has issued the certificate of incorporation, the company secretary should enter the subscribers' names in the register of members.[6]

Section 7 of the Companies Act 1948 required the maximum permitted number of members of a company limited by guarantee to be registered at Companies House. The articles of some older companies will, therefore,

---

1   See Chapter 2.
2   See Chapter 6.
3   See **4.7**.
4   See **2.7**; in a company limited by guarantee and having a share capital, the members may also have subscribed for shares in the company and the amounts paid up and payable on the shares also represent funds available to the creditors on a winding up: Insolvency Act 1986, s 74(3).
5   Companies Act 1985, s 277 and see **6.3**.
6   There may of course be a single subscriber: see s 3A of the Companies Act 1985.

still contain a maximum number of members but this can be removed by a special resolution[1] and there is no need to include a provision to this effect in the articles of a new company.

3.1.3   Companies, minors and bankrupts

A company may, in principle, be a member of a company limited by guarantee just as in a company limited by shares,[2] although the articles may not allow admission of companies as members.[3] A person who is under 18 may be a member of a company limited by guarantee, but the contract constituted by the articles is voidable at the option of the minor before his eighteenth birthday or within a reasonable time afterwards.[4] Unless and until the minor avoids the contract, the minor has all the rights of a member. However, it is open to a company limited by guarantee to disqualify minors from membership or to require them to produce some form of parental approval. This could be important where the company intends to levy substantial subscriptions or membership fees, since the minor's parents could be required to guarantee the payment of the fees. Likewise, the articles of a company limited by guarantee may provide that a bankrupt may not be a member or may be disqualified from membership on becoming bankrupt. As a matter of law, a bankrupt may be a member and may exercise his vote, although any benefits or distributions which are incidental to membership vest in the trustee in bankruptcy, and the bankrupt should vote in accordance with the wishes of his trustee.[5]

3.2   PROCEDURE FOR ADMISSION AS A MEMBER

3.2.1   The application form

Section 22(2) of the Companies Act 1985 deals with the case of members who are not subscribers. A person must agree to become a member and his name must be entered in the register of members before he becomes a member of the company. This means that until a person's name is entered in the register of members, he cannot exercise his vote and has no right to receive notice of, or to attend, meetings. The articles will normally provide that agreement to become a member is effected either by signing the register of members, or by applying for membership in any form settled by the articles or approved by the board. If the company's membership is likely

---

1   See **2.11**.
2   Although note that the effect of creating groups involving companies limited by guarantee may not be the same for tax purposes: *South Shore Mutual Insurance Co Ltd v Blair (Inspector of Taxes)* [1999] STC (SCD) 296.
3   See below.
4   The statements here relating to minors represent English law and not Scots law.
5   The principles relating to corporate members depend on the type of insolvency proceedings.

to become substantial, it is sensible to use an application form rather than rely on signature of the register of members. Signature of the register may be adequate in the case of a property management company, for example, where the register can be kept in the management office.

A sample application form is set out at Appendix C. An application form should contain the name of the company and preferably expressly state that the member agrees to be bound by the provisions of the memorandum and the articles. This serves the purpose of reminding the member of the implications of membership. It may also be advisable for the form to include a statement of the guarantee as set out in the memorandum,[1] which serves to answer the prospective member's next question: what am I liable for? Appendix C also includes a note which explains to the member the implications of joining a company limited by guarantee.

3.2.2 The criteria for admission

The articles should, ideally, contain provisions setting out the criteria for the admission of members. In the case of a company which is to be registered as a charity, the basic premise is that membership must be open to anyone coming to the company with a reasonable application. In other words, it would be permissible for the company to refuse to admit a prospective member whose application was not made in good faith, or whose admission would be likely to be contrary to the interests of the charity. In other cases there seems to be no reason why the articles should not restrict the membership as much as the promoters require, although some restrictions may affect the company's ability to register a name containing a sensitive word.[2] The position may well be different in the case of an alteration to the articles, particularly if it has the effect of excluding existing members.[3]

In the case of a company limited by guarantee that has been set up to promote a particular field of activity, it would be usual for the articles to state that membership is open to anyone with an interest in the particular activity. Alternatively there may be specific criteria: for example, holding membership of another professional body or holding a particular qualification, being resident or (in the case of corporate members) having a place of business in a particular area, or being a particular type of organisation. The articles may provide for prospective members to be nominated by other members, or by a particular class of members, or even by an outside body such as a professional organisation. The articles should set out a procedure for nomination for membership, and should distinguish this from admission, which may (depending on the terms of the articles) be an activity of the company in general meeting, by the board of directors or by a committee of the board.

---

1   See **2.7**.
2   See **2.3.4**.
3   See **3.9.2**.

3.2.3 Discrimination

A company must not discriminate, in the rules relating to eligibility for admission as a member, or in the application of those rules, on grounds of sex, race, physical or mental capacity; although there are specific exemptions for charitable companies set up to further the interests of persons of either gender or of a particular race or religion, and for charities conferring benefits by reference to physical or mental incapacity. In the sex and race discrimination legislation there are special exemptions for companies with less than 25 members that are not trade unions or associations of workers, trade associations or employers' associations or professional bodies.[1] Corporate members may be admitted if, on a construction of the articles, legal persons as well as natural persons (individuals) are eligible for membership. Therefore, if it is desired to exclude corporations from membership then the articles should expressly state that membership is open to individuals rather than to 'persons'.

3.3 TRADE ASSOCIATIONS AND COMPETITION LAW

3.3.1 EC competition law

Article 81 of the EC Treaty[2] prohibits agreements or arrangements between undertakings which have the object or effect of restricting or preventing trade between Member States, subject to clearance procedures. 'Undertaking' is broadly interpreted to mean any business, whether or not it operates with a view to making a profit,[3] though organisations without commercial objectives will not be regarded as undertakings for this purpose. Article 81 can also apply to decisions of trade associations and the constitution of a trade association can be a 'decision' for this purpose.[4] Binding and non-binding recommendations of trade associations (or their directors) to their members may also be treated as agreements between undertakings even though they are unilateral. Trade association activities may also infringe Article 82[5] of the EC Treaty, which prohibits the abuse of a dominant position in the common market. For breaches of the competition rules, fines based on turnover can be imposed upon the trade association itself, its members, or both.

Where membership of a trade association is, in practice if not in law, a requirement of practising a particular trade, European competition law has sought to control the manner in which a member is admitted to the

---

1   See generally: Race Relations Act 1976, ss 11, 25, 34–37; Sex Discrimination Act 1975, ss 12, 43; Disability Discrimination Act 1995, ss 10–16.
2   Formerly Article 85, until the renumbering effected by the 1997 Treaty of Amsterdam.
3   *Interpar v GVL* [1981] OJ L 370/49.
4   Commission Decision (80/917/EEC) *National Sulphuric Acid Association* [1980] OJ L260/24, [1980] 3 CMLR 429; *London Sugar Futures Market* [1985] OJ L369/25.
5   Formerly Article 86.

association. The criteria for admission to the association should be clear and objective, should be legitimate for the functions to be carried out by the trade association and should be proportionate. The admission criteria should not operate in practice so as to exclude a proportion of the market participants (for example, by requiring that the members should keep a certain level of goods in stock). The requirement that the criteria for admission should be objective means that it is unlikely to be appropriate for admission to be controlled by a majority or unanimity of the existing members. The requirement that the application be approved by the board of directors should not contravene this principle if the function of the board's approval is merely to establish whether or not a particular applicant fulfils the published admission criteria.

If the trade association has any effect on trade between Member States of the EU (and in the case of a national association the threshold set by this test is a low one) then its membership criteria should not discriminate between nationals of Member States in terms of the eligibility for or terms of admission to membership, although a requirement that the member should be doing business in the UK is acceptable.

3.3.2 UK competition law

British law formerly had no general policy on the competition law implications of admission to membership of a trade association. The question was whether there were restrictions which contravened the Restrictive Trade Practices Act 1976 (s 6 in the case of goods and s 11 in the case of services). Bona fide subscriptions to trade associations, banded according to turnover, were given specific exemption. The 1976 Act was repealed by the Competition Act 1998 which largely adopts European competition law and applies it to agreements and practices which may have an appreciable effect on trade within the UK, or undertakings whose market share is sufficient that they may be able to abuse a dominant position in the market.[1] In the case of the Chapter I prohibition, the Director General of Fair Trading may impose penalties for breaches of the Competition Act of up to 10% of UK turnover for a maximum of three years, subject to a right of appeal. In addition, the Director General of Fair Trading has far-reaching powers of investigation.

The Competition Act 1998 requires that the criteria for admission are appied in an open and non-discriminatory way. The Office of Fair Trading guidelines state that this may require that there should be an appeal procedure in cases of refusal of admission to the company. Trade associations must not fix their prices or prevent members from poaching customers from each other. Raising standards to be applied across the

---

1   The principles of UK competition law that apply to trade associations are helpfully summarised in the booklet OFT 408: *The Competition Act 1998: Trade Associations, Professions and Self-Regulatory Bodies* (March 1999), available from the OFT and the website www.oft.gov.uk.

board will usually be acceptable as in the best interests of the customers. Quality marks, standard terms and conditions and the exchange of information may all contravene competition law if there is an element of compulsion by the company and if they are not objectively justifiable.

An agreement may be granted individual or block exemptions, if it can be shown to improve production or distribution or to promote technical or economic progress and the restrictions imposed are not disproportionate and do not allow the members significantly to reduce competition in their particular market.[1] In addition, there are some exemptions for designated professional rules of certain professions listed in Sch 4 to the Competition Act 1998.

3.4   WHO MAY ADMIT MEMBERS?

In the absence of any express provision, the power to refuse or to allow an individual to be admitted membership of the company may be exercised by the members of the company, unless on a construction of the clause dealing with the power of the directors, control of entry to membership is given to the directors. Nevertheless, if it is desired that members must be admitted at a general meeting of the company then this should be stated expressly, in the interests of clarity. It would be unwise to place the admission of new members in the hands of the existing members if the membership is likely to reduce to one, since if that member ceases to be capable of acting, for whatever reason, then there will be deadlock. Unless the intention is for the number of members to be serverely limited, it is sensible to give this power to the board (or even a committee of the board), as procedures for calling and holding board meetings are more flexible and meetings tend to be more frequent.[2]

There is no duty on the board (or other admissions body) to give reasons for refusing to admit an individual as a member to a company limited by guarantee unless this is expressly required by the articles. The power to admit members is one which must be exercised in good faith and in the interests of the company. It would be advisable for the reasons for a refusal to admit to be noted in the board minutes, which the members do not have a right to inspect, but which, when signed, form evidence of proceedings at the board meeting.[3]

---

1   Competition Act 1998, s 9.
2   See Chapter 5.
3   See **5.7.6**.

3.5 MEMBERSHIP FEES

The articles may provide for a member to pay a joining fee or an ongoing membership fee but this is not essential. The charging of membership fees may, however, be a useful means for a company limited by guarantee to generate income. If the fee is to be ongoing then the basis on which the renewals are to be due should be stated in the articles. Note that if the company is VAT-registered, membership subscriptions may be subject to VAT if they are consideration for a VATable supply by the company. A new exemption applies to subscriptions to non-profit-making organisations of a political, religious, patriotic, philosophical, philanthropic or civic nature.[1]

If provisions allowing the charging of membership fees are not inserted into the articles on the incorporation of the company, it is still possible to alter the articles to introduce such a fee by passing a special resolution. The new fee will bind existing members.[2] It is not, however, possible to introduce a membership fee without altering the articles, unless every member of the company agrees to the change. In addition, if the articles are not changed it would also be necessary to introduce the payment of the fee as a contractual term incorporated into the agreement formed on the admission of new members, as otherwise a new member would be entitled to assume that the terms on which he would be admitted to membership would be set out as a complete code in the articles. A contractual term of this sort would have to be incorporated before the contract with the company is made. The member should be informed of the level of the fee and the duration of membership gained by paying it before signing the application form (if any) or putting forward the request for admission.

Membership fees may also properly be the subject of by-laws, provided that the article permitting the by-law clearly states how fees are to be introduced.[3]

3.6 THE REGISTER OF MEMBERS

3.6.1 The content and form of the register

A company has a duty to maintain a register of members.[4] The register must contain the names and addresses of the members, the date on which each person was registered as a member, and the date on which any person ceased to be a member. If there is more than one class of members, the register must show, alongside the name and address of the member, the

---

1 See Customs and Excise VAT Information Sheet 11/99, December 1999.
2 *Allen v Gold Reefs of West Africa* [1900] 1 Ch 656, CA.
3 See **2.12.7** on the drafting and use of by-laws.
4 Companies Act 1985, s 352.

class to which that member belongs.[1] There is a fine and a daily default fine for non-compliance with these requirements, which may be levied from the company and from every officer in default. The register of members is rebuttable evidence of the matters which by the Companies Act 1985 are directed or authorised to be entered in it.[2]

Former members should not be immediately removed from the register of members. A former member may only be removed from the register after 20 years from the date on which he ceased to be a member.[3] If there are more than 50 members, the company must keep with the register some form of index which must be kept up to date to match the entries in the register. Alternatively, the register of members may be kept on a computer, provided that the register can be inspected[4] and that the registrar of companies is notified on form G353a.

3.6.2 Single-member companies

If the company has only one member, the company secretary should write in the register of members, next to the name and address of the sole member: 'The company has only one member, with effect from (date)'. If the company has only one member on incorporation, the date included should be the date shown on the certificate of incorporation. If the company gains additional members, the company secretary should write in the register of members next to the name and address of the former sole member: 'The company ceased to have only one member on (date)'. The relevant date will be the date on which the second member's name was entered into the register of members. The company and its officers may be fined for failing to comply with this requirement.

3.6.3 Where should the register of members be kept?

The register of members should be kept at the registered office of the company. However, if the work of making up the register is done somewhere else (such as the offices of the company's solicitor or accountant), the register may be kept at that other place, provided that form G353 is filed notifying the address to the registrar of companies. Form G353 should also be used to notify any change in the location of the register. There is no need to file form G353 if the register has only ever been kept at the registered office.

3.6.4 Inspection of the register

A company's register of members (together with any index of names) must generally be open for inspection by any member of the company without

---

1   Companies Act 1985, s 352(4).
2   Companies Act 1985, s 361.
3   Companies Act 1985, s 352(6).
4   See **3.6.4**.

charge. A person who is not a member must be allowed to inspect the register but the company may if it wishes charge a small fee for this (currently £2.50 per hour or part of an hour during which the right to inspect is exercised).[1] The only permitted exception to the right of inspection is that a company may close its register of members for up to 30 days each year, but must announce the closure period in a newspaper circulating in the district in which the company's registered office is situated.[2]

The register must be open for at least two hours between the hours of 9am and 5pm on each 'business day'. The term 'business day' is defined in the regulations and excludes weekends and bank holidays. The company is not obliged to provide photocopying facilities but it must allow the person inspecting the register to copy the information by means of taking notes or transcribing the register. The presentation of the register of members is not required to be in a manner which groups together entries by reference to, for example, a geographical area of registered addresses; nationality; natural or legal persons; or gender. In other words, if a person inspecting the register wishes to find this information, he will have to read through the entire register and extract the relevant information from each individual entry.

Any person may request a copy of the register or any part of it, on payment of a fee. This is currently £2.50 for up to 100 entries, £20 for the next 1000 entries (or part of 1000) and £15 for every subsequent 1000 or part of 1000. The company must comply with the request within 10 days, beginning on the date on which the request is received by the company. This right to request copies is separate from the right to inspect. So if a person inspects the register and prefers to pay for copies to be provided rather than transcribe the entries, the company may demand a further fee and has 10 days to provide the copies. The section refers to the copies being 'sent' within this time which must mean that the copies must be posted within 10 days, rather than that they must reach the person who requested them within that time.

3.6.5 Mistakes in the register of members

If the company secretary makes a mistake in the register of members, or if the register is lost or destroyed, the company may not correct the error or recreate the register. This can be done only by the court, for example under the power given in s 359 of the Companies Act 1985. In addition to ordering the rectification of the register, the court may order that the company should pay damages to any person aggrieved. This is most likely to arise, in the case of a company limited by guarantee, if the company makes a distribution to its members, and a person who should have been entered in the register loses out because his name has been omitted. It has recently

---

1   Companies (Inspection and Copying of Registers, Indices and Documents) Regulations 1991, SI 1991/1998.
2   Companies Act 1985, s 358.

been confirmed, however, that the s 359 procedure is inappropriate for the determination of substantial issues of fact.[1]

3.6.6   Membership certificates

A company limited by shares is obliged to issue share certificates to each shareholder.[2] A company limited by guarantee is not under any equivalent obligation except where it has a share capital and allots shares. Neither does the provision apply which states that a share certificate is evidence of title to a share.[3] However, companies limited by guarantee can and do issue membership certificates, and care should be taken to issue these correctly, as if a certificate is shown to be an authorised document produced by the company, it would be regarded as evidence that a person is entitled to be entered in the register of members. The company, having issued the certificate, would be prevented from subsequently denying the holder's membership, provided that the holder was the person named on the certificate. Certificates are also often regarded by members as valuable in themselves, for a variety of reasons.

The certificate should reflect the name of the member as shown in the register of members, and should indicate the class of membership (if applicable). It should be sealed and attested as provided by the articles of association, or executed without a seal as provided in the Companies Act 1985.[4]

3.7   CESSATION OF MEMBERSHIP

3.7.1   Retirement

It is common for the articles to provide that a member may retire from the company by giving notice to the company; and if the articles provide a procedure for retirement, it must be followed. What is the position in the absence of such a provision? Would retirement constitute a breach of contract by the member, and if so would the company be able to claim as damages the amount of any membership fees which would otherwise be payable? Sometimes the articles of a company limited by guarantee will provide that a member may retire provided that there remain at least two other members (or some higher number of members). This was necessary when a company could not have a single member, but its only function now is to prevent the membership of a company falling below the level which is set as the quorum for a general meeting.

---

1   *Keene v Martin* (1999) *The Times*, November 11.
2   Companies Act 1985, s 185.
3   Companies Act 1985, s 186.
4   Companies Act 1985, s 36A (England and Wales) or s 36B (Scotland).

In an unincorporated association, a member may always retire by giving notice if the rules of the club are silent on the point.[1] As a general principle of contract law, a party to a contract may terminate a contract on reasonable notice if the parties have not agreed specific termination or expiry provisions. Since the articles are a form of contract, this principle should apply to companies limited by guarantee, except that it is uncertain how further aspects of contract law would apply. For example, would a member be entitled to any refund of membership fees? Conversely, would the company have a claim for any unpaid membership fees which had fallen due at the date of resignation, or which would have become due had the member not resigned? Probably the general principles of contract construction would be applied to the articles.

3.7.2 Cessation in other circumstances

Articles will also commonly provide for membership to cease automatically on the happening of certain events. For example: on death; bankruptcy; the making of an order under the mental health legislation; or upon conviction of an offence punishable by imprisonment. If admission to membership depends on membership of another organisation or the holding of a professional qualification then logically the loss of that other membership or qualification should be a ground for removal, although it would be a matter of construction whether the cessation of membership of the company is automatic in those circumstances.[2] Articles may also provide for membership to cease if a membership fee is not paid when due. However, since the intentions of a member who fails to pay a subscription may not be clear (for example, it may be a genuine oversight), it would be preferable for this to provide grounds for removal of the member rather than for it to amount to automatic disqualification with no right of appeal. This would effectively mean giving the company the right to terminate the contract for the breach of a fundamental term. The articles may also provide for the member to be removed in certain circumstances, but care should be taken in the drafting and application of articles of this nature.[3]

3.8 TRANSFER OF MEMBERSHIP

Many companies limited by guarantee provide that membership is not transferable and ceases on death (or, in the case of corporate members, on winding up or insolvency). It is not the case that membership is never transferable; everything depends on the construction of the articles. Membership is a bundle of contractual rights and those rights are therefore assignable on general contractual principles. Where the contract provides for a method of transfer, this procedure should be followed.

---

1   *Finch v Oake* [1896] 1 Ch 409.
2   See **3.9**.
3   See Appendix A.

Particular considerations apply to the transfer of membership of a trade association. Whether or not membership of a trade association requires the payment of a substantial admission or membership fee, membership will be a valuable asset of the member. It may, therefore, be appropriate for membership to be transferable, in order to avoid any implication that the articles of the company, which can be a 'decision' of the undertaking for competition law purposes,[1] are anti-competitive.

3.9   EXPULSION OF MEMBERS

3.9.1   Express provisions for expulsion

The articles of a company limited by guarantee may provide a procedure for the expulsion of members from the company, or they may authorise the creation of rules or by-laws to regulate the process. Alternatively, the articles may leave the removal of members to the discretion of the board of directors. Any power to expel given to the board must be exercised bona fide in the interests of the company. If the expulsion is to be voted upon by the members, it is not known whether the majority owe any duty, in exercising their vote, to the minority being expelled, other than where natural justice applies.[2]

3.9.2   Expulsion without express provision

If there is no provision for the expulsion of a member, but no express prohibition on expulsion, can the company validly expel a member? It is safest to assume that a company may never expel a member without an express power to do so. Even if the position is analysed in contractual terms,[3] the position is far from certain. An expulsion of a member could be viewed as a termination of the contract by one party, namely the company, in the absence of an express termination clause. In contract law, contracts without termination clauses may be held to be terminable on reasonable notice if, in the light of the evidence, the intention of the parties when the contract was formed could be said to be that the contract should not last forever.[4] The courts have implied termination clauses into contracts of employment and in contracts for the supply of services on this basis, but it seems unlikely that a court would be persuaded to construe a contract of membership as having a termination clause, unless it was clear from the other terms of the memorandum and articles that membership was subject to certain ongoing conditions, such as the member practising a particular trade or profession. Even non-payment of an annual subscription may not be enough to confer an implied power to expel, since the necessary remedy

1   See **3.3**.
2   *Clemens v Clemens Bros Ltd* [1976] 2 All ER 268.
3   As the memorandum and articles form a contract between the members and the company: Companies Act 1985, s 14(1).
4   *Winter Garden Theatre (London) Ltd v Millennium Productions Ltd* [1948] AC 173, HL.

would be a claim for a debt owed to the company by the member. If there is a power to expel, the same uncertainties relating to rights to refunds of subscriptions apply as in the case of retirement (see **3.7.1**).

A related question concerns alterations to the articles which have the effect of removing a member. In *Sidebottom v Kershaw, Leese & Co,*[1] the court considered a special resolution passed by a quasi-partnership company limited by shares, altering the articles to allow the directors to require any shareholder who competed with the company to transfer his shares at full value to a nominee of the directors. It was held that, since the power could have validly been inserted in the articles registered on formation of the company, the alteration would be valid if it was made in good faith in the interests of the company as a whole. On the facts, the alteration was held to be made in good faith. This case may provide authority for alterations to the articles which confer on the board of a company limited by guarantee the power to expel a member, but it is doubtful whether it would authorise alterations designed to remove a particular member.[2]

3.9.3   Natural justice

The common law principles of natural justice may require procedural fairness where a body or an individual has a power to make a decision which will affect the legitimate interests of an individual. The principles have no impact on the substantive fairness of the decision: in other words, if an organisation reaches an unfair decision by a fair procedure, the principles will not apply. In the case of a company limited by guarantee, the principle may apply in cases of expulsion from membership. If applicable, the principles of natural justice give the expelled member the right to know the charges made against him, and the right to be heard in his own defence by an unbiased tribunal.

The principles of natural justice are usually applied to cases where there is a decision made by a public body which has adversely affected the rights of an individual, and that decision is judicially reviewed.[3] However, the principles pre-date the introduction of the application for judicial review; they applied to overturn decisions made by magistrates following irregular procedures, and in cases of deprivation of office. In the nineteenth century, certain of the principles were applied to professional bodies and unincorporated clubs in the exercise of their disciplinary functions.[4]

---

1   [1920] 1 Ch 154, CA.
2   *Clemens v Clemens Bros Ltd* [1976] 2 All ER 268.
3   See **1.7.3**.
4   *Dawkins v Antrobus* (1881) 17 ChD 615.

3.9.4 Limits on the application of the principles of natural justice

Should the fact that a body is incorporated mean that the principles of natural justice do not apply? This question was considered by Megarry J in *Gaiman v National Association for Mental Health*.[1] The association, a company limited by guarantee, was formed under the Companies Act 1929. It came under the scrutiny of the court as a result of a motion for an interlocutory injunction made by a member who was a Scientologist. The Association had a dispute with Scientologists concerning the practice of psychiatry, which had led to accusations of libel. The Association became the subject of what Counsel for the Association called a 'take-over bid': there was a dramatic increase in the number of applications for member-ship, and it appeared that most of the additional applications were from Scientologists. The new members then made nominations to the board for the elections to be held at the annual general meeting, as they were entitled to do under the articles. Under the articles, there was a power given to the board to request a member to resign and if the member did not resign there was an appeal to the company in general meeting. The board wrote to 302 admitted members who were known to be or who were suspected of being Scientologists, requesting their resignation, in order to prevent the take-over bid. The members were not told why the board wanted them to resign and were not given the chance to make representations at a hearing.

Megarry J held that the principles of natural justice did not apply to the board's decision, although he admitted that it was a difficult case and he did not have any precedent to rely on. His reasons were as follows.

(1) The board's power to expel was one that had to be exercised in the best interests of the company and that required speed, which was inconsist-ent with the principles of natural justice which would have required the Association to give the Scientologists a hearing. It was not an improper exercise of the directors' powers to require the resignation of those holding antithetical views and who were about to make a bid to secure control of the company.

(2) Even where there was an element of 'expropriation', where the boards of companies limited by shares had applied articles allowing compul-sory share transfers, the courts had held that the principles did not apply. The case for the principles applying to companies limited by guarantee was, therefore, even weaker.

(3) The wording of the article in question militated against the application of natural justice, since it was not confined to cases of misconduct. If the power to expel had been limited to cases of misconduct, the question of reputation would have been at stake (as in many of the 'club' cases) and the principles might apply.

---

1   [1971] Ch 317.

Megarry J also rejected an argument by Counsel that the fact of incorporation should not affect the applicability of natural justice; ie that the company should be treated as analogous to a club, rather than treated as if it were a company limited by shares. The judge held that Parliament had created statutory rules for the running of companies which were not applicable to members of unincorporated clubs, and the members of a company were also protected by the existence of directors' duties. The judge held that incorporation was a change of substance of the entity and so the rules which applied to the unincorporated body did not necessarily apply to the corporate body. However, it could also be argued that had Parliament intended that the members of a company limited by guarantee (or indeed a company limited by shares) should have no protection given by the rules of natural justice then it would have legislated to this effect, or created a statutory code dealing with the procedure for expelling a member.

The case is a first instance decision and its scope is not clear from the cases in which it has been cited. Megarry J admitted that a motion for an interlocutory judgment was not the place for a full discussion of the law. It is possible that where the decision could affect the livelihood or reputation of a member, the court would apply the principles of the club cases by analogy. The exceptional case is where the articles of association (or, possibly, other rules of the company adopted pursuant to the constitution) disapply the principles of natural justice; but where natural justice applies, the court is likely to be slow to find that the principles have effectively been excluded by contract.[1]

The *Gaiman* case could be confined to its facts. First, the best interests of the company required a speedy decision. The judge's decision was that it was not in the best interests of the company that the Scientologists should be able to be elected to the board. However, on other facts this criteria might not apply: rarely will an expulsion case concern so many members expelled at once and for the same reason. The case may be confined to cases where there is a 'take-over bid' in the sense used by Counsel. This might occur, for example, in a 'carpetbagging'[2] scenario. The courts have always recognised that natural justice may be modifed in emergency situations, such as where the conduct of a member threatens the activities of the other members in some way.

Secondly, the wording of the clause was interpreted as giving the board a wide discretion as to the expulsion of a member. Where there is no emergency situation, and where the expulsion of the member could imply an allegation of misconduct, or the expulsion affects the ability of the member to practise his trade or profession, it is submitted that *Gaiman* should not be used as an authority for denying the member a right to a hearing. There is, however, little guidance from the cases as to exactly what that right entails. Ideally, the question of the members' rights should be

---

1   See for example *Lee v Showman's Guild of Great Britain* [1952] 1 All ER 1175, CA.
2   See **1.10**.

addressed in the articles themselves (or in rules made under the articles, provided these are properly incorporated into the statutory contract)[1] and if it is desired that no member who is expelled from the company should be given a statement of the reasons for the expulsion, and should in no circumstances be entitled to be heard in his own defence or to have an appeal, this policy should be set out in full in clear wording. In addition to this being a strong deterrent against a member attempting to take issue with the expulsion, it may also persuade the court that the member had voluntarily accepted the provisions of the articles as a term of the contract for membership. In Megarry J's terms, the contract for membership would continue until terminated, but termination could be effected at any time by the procedure set out in the articles.

However, the jurisdiction of the court can never be completely ousted, and whether or not natural justice applies, there remains the principle of company law, applied in *Gaiman*, that the board's power to expel should be exercised in good faith in the best interests of the company as a whole. Therefore, the board cannot use the power to expel in order to settle private disputes, or out of malice, or to swing the vote at a general meeting.

3.9.5 Expulsion of members of trade associations

Aside from the principles of natural justice, there may be competition law reasons for providing a procedure for expulsion of a member of a trade association rather than making this a discretionary procedure. The European Commission Decision *Gema*[2] concerned the expulsion of a member from a collecting society. It was held that the board of directors should give the member the opportunity to make representations, and must give reasons for its decision. There must be an appropriate appeal procedure and, in some cases, the member must be able to challenge the expulsion decision in court.

3.10 THE NATURE OF THE MEMBERSHIP RIGHTS

3.10.1 General rights and obligations

Membership of a company limited by guarantee can be thought of as membership of a club which has corporate form. The members have rights and obligations by virtue of their membership. The sources of these rights and obligations are:

– the memorandum and articles of association;
– general company law; and

---

1   See Appendix A2.
2   (71/224/EEC) OJ [1971] L 134/15, [1971] CMLR D35.

– any rules or by-laws which may be prescribed by the company from time to time.

There may also, exceptionally, be obligations which the members accept outside the corporate structure.[1]

The nature of the relationship between the company, its members, and its board of directors will vary with the type of company, and the nature of the provisions of the memorandum and articles. In the case of a property management company, for example, the members may be concerned only to see that the correct procedures are followed for the setting of the level of management charge and that they are provided with satisfactory accounts. The company is simply a vehicle for the collective ownership and management of the properties and in reality is part and parcel of the landlord and tenant relationship. Equally, in the case of a mutual assurance organisation the corporate structure and the opportunities it offers in terms of pooling of property and risk are the most significant features of the relationship. In the case of a trade association, however, the role of the members may be very significant and the membership of the company not just incidental to property ownership but an important part of the members' livelihoods.

In the case of all these types of company, the common feature is that the relationship in company law terms between the various groups within a company remains the same. The general management of the company is normally entrusted to the directors, but the members have the more important role in terms of making decisions about fundamental aspects of the company: its constitution; the composition of its board of directors; winding up; or changing the company's name.

3.10.2 Distribution of profits

A company limited by guarantee may distribute profits to its members if there is nothing in the memorandum or articles prohibiting this. Every company has, in the absence of an express provision, the implied power to distribute dividends. The rules governing the legality of dividends are contained in ss 263 to 281 of the Companies Act 1985.[2] In the case of a company which is to be a charity, there must be a 'no-distribution' clause and the same is true of a company which wishes to omit the word 'limited' from its name.[3] No company limited by guarantee may allow a person a right to participate in the divisible profits of the company otherwise than as a member.[4] This last prohibition does not prevent different classes of members having different entitlements either in the life of the company or

---

1   An example is the collection of obligations under rules relating to the use of a collective trade mark adopted by the company: s 49 of the Trade Marks Act 1994.
2   See Chapter 6.
3   See **2.3.7**.
4   Companies Act 1985, s 15(1).

on a winding up, since they still participate as members. It is designed to prevent the creation of a share capital in a company limited by guarantee.

If the memorandum or articles do permit distributions, either during the life of the company as dividends, or on winding up the company, then members for the time being can be said to have an interest in the assets of the company and the duties of the directors include the obligation to act in the best interests of the company and not to prejudice that interest. Although on questions of statutory interpretation it may be convenient to treat each member as having a share in the company,[1] their interest in the company cannot be 'property' if it cannot be alienated (ie transferred to another person). Where the articles of a company limited by guarantee permit membership to be transferred (as is sometimes the case in trade associations, for example), the rights of members are closer to property interests, although these organisations are normally constituted on a not-for-profit basis.

3.10.3   The nature of rights where distributions are prohibited

Where the members of a company limited by guarantee do not have any property interest in the company, the nature of their rights is, in reality, different to that found in a company limited by shares.[2] If the company is prohibited from making distributions by its constitution (usually by the memorandum, but this provision could legally be included in the articles), then the members' rights are limited to rights to vote. The members may, by their vote, be able to control what happens to property (for example, on winding up, the memorandum may permit the members to choose the organisation that is to benefit from the remaining assets of the company) but they cannot appropriate the property to themselves. This distinction between the two types of membership rights may be relevant when it comes to considering whether the directors have acted in the best interests of the company, or whether the interests of a minority have been unfairly prejudiced.[3]

3.11   CLASS RIGHTS

3.11.1   What are class rights?

We normally think of class rights as rights attaching to a class of shares. Shares will commonly have both a nominal value and a class or description (ordinary £1 shares, 50p preferences shares and so on). If the memorandum or articles of the company describe by reference to a particular class the

---

1   See eg *Re National Farmers' Union Development Trust Ltd* [1972] 1 WLR 1548, [1973] 1 All ER 135.
2   It is possible for the memorandum of a company limited by shares to include a no-distribution clause, but that rare case is not considered here.
3   See **4.5.8**.

rights attaching to shares in that class, then ss 125 to 127 of the Companies Act 1985 restrict the ability of the company in general meeting to authorise variations of those rights. A more detailed discussion of the class rights rules applying to companies limited by shares is beyond the scope of this book; but note that in a company limited by guarantee and having a share capital, ss 125 to 127 will apply to the extent that the shares are divided into classes.

In a company limited by guarantee which is intended to have a broad membership (for example, a trade association), there are commonly classes or categories of membership. For example, full membership may be open to people who have a certain qualification or practice a certain trade, and there may be associate membership available for interested observers. Classes of membership may also be used in fairly small companies where there is a need to distinguish between, for example, founder members and new members. If the rights of the members vary between the classes, those rights are regarded as class rights. The obligation to pay a particular level of membership fee, or any other distinction between the types of member which does not confer some right or benefit on the members, is not a class right. Class rights commonly relate to matters which are equally important to members of a company limited by guarantee as they are to shareholders, such as the election of directors. There may be class rights in a company limited by guarantee which would not be found in a company limited by shares, such as rights incidental to procedures for expulsion from a membership, or to the refund or transfer of a membership fee. Although ss 125 to 127 do not apply to a company which does not have a share capital, the common law rules which applied before those sections were introduced[1] continue to apply to companies limited by guarantee. A particular consequence is that the remedy under s 127 of the Companies Act 1985, given to shareholders who object to variations, does not apply to companies limited by guarantee. Neither does the remedy conferred under s 17(1),[2] since the authority for the variation is given by common law and not by that section. The only remedy available to the aggrieved member would be an action under ss 459 to 461 of the Companies Act 1985.[3]

3.11.2   The common law class rights rules

(1) If the class rights are contained in the articles (or otherwise, for example in by-laws or rules) and the articles contain a clause governing the variation of class rights, then that clause must be followed, even if the language of the clause is permissive rather than restrictive.

---

1   By the Companies Act 1980.
2   See **2.8.1**.
3   See **4.5.9**.

(2) If the class rights are contained in the articles and the articles do not contain a clause governing the variation of the rights, then s 9 of the Companies Act 1985 will apply and the articles may be altered by a special resolution without the need for the holding of class meetings.

(3) If the class rights are contained in the memorandum, and the memorandum has a variation clause, that clause must be followed.

(4) If the class rights are contained in the memorandum and there is no variation clause in the memorandum, the class rights cannot be varied, although there is some authority[1] to the effect that if the articles as originally registered on incorporation included a variation clause, this clause could in principle permit variation of the clause in the memorandum.

3.11.3   Notifying Companies House of class rights

Note that although ss 125 to 127 of the Companies Act 1985 do not apply to companies limited by guarantee, s 129 of the Act specifically applies to companies not having a share capital. This section requires registration of the 'prescribed particulars' of any class rights that are created otherwise than in the memorandum or articles or by means of a resolution that is required to be registered at Companies House. Where class rights are created by rules or by-laws, or by the terms of a contract under which a member is admitted, a form 129(1) must be completed. There are also forms required if class rights are varied other than by an alteration to the memorandum or articles[2] or if a name or designation is given or changed.[3] Class rights in a company limited by guarantee cannot, therefore, be kept secret by keeping them outside the articles.

3.12   THE CHALLENGE OF A WIDER MEMBERSHIP

3.12.1   Property management or mutual assurance companies

In a property management or mutual assurance company, the membership of the company will be limited to those who have an equal interest in the sharing of risk or the management of the property. It would be inappropriate to broaden the membership. In the case of a company which is a charity, the basic principle is that membership of the company must be open to anyone with a reasonable application. This does not mean that that the company must actively encourage applications and it is perfectly possible for a charity to be efficiently run within the law if the membership is, in practice, limited to the trustees. There may still be individuals or groups of

---

1   The Scottish cases: *Oban Distilleries Ltd* (1903) 5 F 11 40, *Marshall Fleming & Co Ltd* (1938) SC 873, which were followed by Parliament in enacting s 125(4).

2   Companies Act 1985, s 129(2).

3   Companies Act 1985, s 129(3).

individuals with opposing interests who each wish to have the major role in dictating the 'policy' of the charity (for example, founder members and new members). The constitution can be designed to avoid conflict between these parties.

3.12.2 Representative and regulatory organisations

In the case of a company limited by guarantee set up to fulfil the needs of a particular interest group, trade, or campaign, or to act as a regulatory organisation, the promoters should address the question of whether a broad membership is desirable. It may be that the interests of democracy are paramount, but a broad membership will have its corresponding share of problems. The board may find it difficult to institute change, for example changes to the memorandum and articles, or to change the procedure by which the directors are appointed. There is always a tension between the needs of efficiency, which dictate that the company should be under the control of the board without the need to refer every question to the members for approval, and the needs of the members of a mutual organisation to see that their interests are accurately reflected in the board's decisions. If the company's constitution puts too much control in the hands of the board, the members may feel that they are excluded from important decisions which may, on many occasions, fundamentally affect their livelihoods.

These tensions may be eased by incorporating into the company's constitution procedures under which the members have input into the decision-making procedure. An example would be for the articles to provide for the election of a members' committee, which would be responsible for the preparation of by-laws. The board could then adopt the by-laws, if authorised by the articles, without the need to refer them to the general meeting for approval. The making of by-laws could thus be seen to be done in a more democratic manner. Care should be taken, however, to ensure that this mechanism does not bring with it the problems associated with 'drafting by committee': the process may be delayed and the rules may be internally inconsistent, representing a compromise between competing interest groups within the membership. An approach which might solve some of these problems would be for the articles to provide that the by-laws should be drafted by (or on behalf of) the board, and then put to the committee for consultation. The board would then take into account the various arguments put forward by the committee, and could then finalise and adopt the draft.

3.12.3 Trade associations with corporate members

Another tension may be revealed in the case of a trade association which admits corporate members. In an industry in which there is a wide variation in the size and economic power of the participants, the company may wish to be representative of the whole industry and, therefore, may set its membership fees or subscriptions at a level which encourges membership among those players at the smaller end of the market. This can, however, lead to an imbalance if the 'one member, one vote' rule is preserved, and the larger players may insist on weighted voting rights. Equally, those caught in the middle may fear spoiling tactics by those with the real power: if any company may be admitted to membership, how should the company deal with the prospect of a large multinational gaining additional votes by nominating all its many dormant subsidiaries to the membership, or even registering multiple subsidiaries for the purpose? There are many ways to deal with these concerns: weighted voting rights,[1] banded membership fees, classes of membership with constitutional roles for each class, associations of small companies as members and tailored membership criteria may all be included in the company's constitution. Those involved in the management of a trade association should, however, be aware that the wider the membership, the more likely are the activities of the company to contravene competition law.[2]

---

1   See **2.11**.
2   See **3.3**.

Chapter 4

DIRECTORS

4.1 SELECTING THE DIRECTORS

4.1.1 Who are the directors?

There is no definition of the term 'director' given in the Companies Act 1985. A person who occupies the position of a director, whatever name he is given, is a director for the purposes of the Act.[1] In a company limited by guarantee, the directors are very often called Governors, Members of the Board of Management, Trustees, or Committee Members. The promoters of a company limited by guarantee should, however, be very clear as to who are the directors of the company and to make sure that the directors are properly appointed and are aware of their duties. For simplicity, in this book the term 'director' is used throughout.

4.1.2 Executive and non-executive directors

There is strictly no distinction in company law between an executive and a non-executive director. However, the term 'executive' is usually reserved for those directors who are employed by the company, and 'non-executive' means those who undertake their directorships in a part-time or supervisory capacity. A non-executive director should, however, be aware that the duty of care which is imposed on directors depends not merely upon the time that they are required to devote to the company's business but also on the functions that they carry out in relation to the company. A person who is expected to supervise, in a non-executive capacity, the executive directors of a company may find that the standard to which he is expected to perform is just as high as that expected of those whom he is supervising. However, the court will, in disqualification proceedings, take account of the fact that a non-executive director is not necessarily in a position to give his full attention to the affairs of the company.[2]

4.1.3 Shadow directors

A shadow director is a person in accordance with whose directions or instructions the directors of a company are accustomed to act. The mere fact that a person gives advice to the directors in a professional capacity does not make that person a shadow director.[3] There is also a list of sections referred to in s 741 of the Companies Act 1985 in which the references to a

---

1   Companies Act 1985, s 741(1).
2   *Re Peppermint Park Ltd* [1998] BCC 23, ChD.
3   Companies Act 1985, s 741(2).

shadow director do not include a parent company whose advice is usually followed by the directors of the subsidiary. Shadow directors may be liable to the same penalties as appointed directors, and in particular, can be disqualified under the Company Directors Disqualification Act 1986. In a recent case concerning the 1986 Act,[1] it was held that the term 'shadow director' in that Act should be widely construed so as to give the maximum protection of the public as intended by the 1986 Act. The 'directions or instructions' given by a shadow director can include (non-professional) advice; the test of whether a person is a shadow director is whether he has a 'real influence' over the company's affairs.

4.1.4   Qualifications

There are no particular qualifications required for being a director, although the Institute of Directors now offers the award of the status of 'chartered director' to members of the IoD who pass an examination in company direction and subscribe to the IoD's Code of Professional Conduct.[2] Directors can, however, be disqualified from holding office, by means of specific statutes.[3] The Company Directors Disqualification Act 1986 also provides for automatic disqualification of undischarged bankrupts, and for disqualification by the court for unfitness and for specific offences.[4] The articles may exclude minors,[5] other companies, or those who are subject to orders under the mental health legislation, from being directors.

4.1.5   Age limits

There is no minimum age in the Companies Act for serving as a director in England and Wales. The Companies House notes for guidance recommend that children under 16 should not be appointed as directors of a company as they are thought not to be able to understand the full implications of company law and their responsibilities under it, or to have the experience necessary to perform the duties of a company director, although the notes indicate that registration staff will consider appointments of those under 16 in exceptional cases. In Scotland, the Registrar will not register the appointment of a director under the age of 16 years, as a child below that age does not have the legal capacity to accept a directorship.[6] In a company limited by guarantee, there is no upper age limit for serving as a director unless the articles provide for this, or if the company is a subsidiary of a public limited company.[7] In the latter case, an ordinary resolution of which

---

1   *Secretary of State for Trade and Industry v Deverell* (2000) *The Times*, January 21, CA.
2   See www.iod.co.uk for details.
3   For example, clergymen are not able to be directors, by virtue of s 29 of the Pluralities Act 1838; an auditor of another company in the same group may not be a director of the company.
4   See **4.9**.
5   Minors are those under 18 in England and Wales and those under 16 in Scotland.
6   Age of Legal Capacity (Scotland) Act 1991.
7   Companies Act 1985, s 293.

special notice has been given is required for the appointment of a director over the age of 70 or for him to remain in office.

4.1.6 Membership qualifications

There is no requirement that a director should be a member of the company unless this is expressly provided in the articles. If under the articles it is a necessary condition of serving as a director that a person should be a member of the company (or perhaps in the case of a company limited by guarantee and having a share capital, hold at least one share in the company), this means the director must be admitted as a member in accordance with the procedures set out in the articles and his name must be entered into the register of members. In drafting the articles, consideration should also be given to provisions to the effect that the director ceases to hold office if his membership lapses; or that membership lapses automatically if the member ceases to be a director.

4.2 APPOINTMENT OF DIRECTORS

4.2.1 Method of appointment

The appointment of the first directors who take office on incorporation is done by the directors signing form 10, which is also signed by or on behalf of the subscribers. Section 10 of the Companies Act 1985 provides that the articles may not appoint a person as director or company secretary unless he is named in form 10. Subsequent appointments of directors are always governed by the articles. The appointment may be by means of an ordinary resolution of the members (with or without a requirement for nomination by an existing director); or directors may be nominees of particular members or classes of members. Appointment may simply be by resolution of the existing board, or even by a single director appointing his successor. Note, however, that s 308 of the Companies Act 1985 provides that if the director is empowered (in the articles or any other contract) to assign his office, this is subject to the approval of a special resolution of the members. This does not apply to the appointment of an alternate director who is not an assignee of the office of director but is an agent of the director who appoints him. Section 285 of the Companies Act 1985 provides that the acts of a director or manager are valid despite any defect which is later discovered in his appointment or qualification. This would, for example, validate the acts of a director required under the articles to have a membership qualification but whose name had not actually been entered into the register of members. However, it cannot be used to cure a complete lack of appointment.[1]

---

1   *Morris v Kanssen* [1946] AC 459.

4.2.2   Publicity for directors' details

The prescribed particulars of all directors (including shadow directors[1] and
alternate directors[2]) appointed must be notified to Companies House on
form 288a. Any changes must be notified on form 288c within 14 days after
the date of the change. The notification is simply a question of filling in a
form (available free of charge from Companies House), but potential
directors should note that they will have to disclose their home addresses
which will be displayed on the public register. Directors will also have to
disclose their date of birth, nationality, business occupation, full names and
former names (there are certain exceptions; for example, a married woman
need not disclose her maiden name). The director must also disclose the full
names of any other companies incorporated in Great Britain of which he is
a director or former director. Again there are permitted exceptions: a
director need not disclose companies of which he ceased to be a director
more than five years ago, nor companies which are dormant. Full details are
set out in s 289 of the Companies Act 1985 and on the form itself. In
addition, these details must be included in the register of directors which
must be kept at the registered office.[3] The register must be open to
inspection by any member of the company without charge; non-members
are also entitled to inspect the register but the company may charge a fee.[4]

The company is not obliged to include any details of directors on its
notepaper, but if any directors are named (other than in the text of the letter
or as its signatory) then all the directors must be named. This includes, in
principle, both executive and non-executive directors, alternate directors[5]
and shadow directors.[6] The directors' forenames (or recognised abbreviations or initials) and surnames must be stated.[7] A summary of the
notepaper requirements is also set out at Appendix E.

4.3   PROVISIONS OF THE ARTICLES OF ASSOCIATION

4.3.1   Maximum and minimum number of directors

The articles may provide for a maximum or minimum number of directors,
or for these to be determined by the company in general meeting. In the
case of a company which is to be registered as a charity, it is usual to provide
that there must be a minimum of three directors, as the Charity Commissioners take the view that a board of one or two does not give an

---

1   See **4.1.3**.
2   See **4.3.4**.
3   Companies Act 1985, s 288(1).
4   The fees and detailed inspection requirements in the case of the register of directors are
     the same as those that apply to the register of members: see **3.6.4**.
5   If the alternate is appointed for all purposes, see **4.3.4**.
6   See **4.1.3**.
7   Companies Act 1985, s 305.

adequate range of opinions on matters to be decided at the meetings of the board. Otherwise, it is not essential to prescribe the maximum or minimum in the articles and there is much to be said for the flexibility of leaving these to be determined as required by the company in general meeting from time to time. If it is intended that there should be a single director at any point, the articles should provide for a quorum of one at board meetings in those circumstances. However, a single director may not also serve as company secretary.

4.3.2 Retirement by rotation

The articles of a company limited by guarantee may provide for the board of directors to be subject to retirement by rotation. Usually, this will take the form of an election being required at every annual general meeting after the first such meeting, at which a proportion (commonly one-third) of the board must retire. The articles will usually provide for those retiring to be eligible for re-election. Unless it is to be compulsory for all the board to retire at each annual general meeting, the articles should deal with the possibility that the number of directors may change and cease to be a multiple of the number who are to retire each year. The articles should also accommodate the possibility that no new directors, or an insufficient number to make the total up to any minimum number prescribed by the articles or required to constitute a quorum, may be appointed. In a charitable company, the Charity Commissioners prefer the board of directors to be subject to retirement by rotation as it is thought to discourage stagnation in the board. The same thinking may apply to a club, a trade association or pressure group.

4.3.3 Additional directors

It is possible for the articles to allow the board of directors to appoint additional directors. Where there is to be rotation of directors, this is usually designed to allow the filling of temporary vacancies. The articles will usually provide for the director appointed (or 'co-opted') by the board to hold office only until the next annual general meeting.

Equally, the articles may reserve to the company in general meeting the ability to appoint additional directors. In the situation where there is no board capable of acting, for example if the number of serving directors falls below the quorum, this provision allows the company to appoint additional directors to make up the numbers and to permit the company to continue operating. In fact, the company in general meeting always has power to appoint an additional director where there is no board capable of acting.[1] The alternative is to provide for this situation expressly, effectively suspending the quorum requirement to allow the reduced board to act for

---

1   *Barron v Potter* [1914] 1 Ch 895.

the purpose of appointing a director to the vacancy but for no other purpose.

4.3.4 Alternate directors

Alternate directors ('alternates') are directors who are appointed to take a director's place at board meetings which he is not able to attend. The power to appoint an alternate can be useful, for example, if a director is likely to be travelling abroad. The appointment of an alternate is permitted only if expressly provided for in the company's articles; usually the articles state that an alternate director is to be nominated by the relevant director and approved by the board.

The provisions of the articles which deal with the appointment of alternates may specify the circumstances in which the alternate should have power to act. The alternate's power may be limited to acting at board meetings. Table A provides that the alternate is appointed 'generally to perform all the functions of his appointor as a director in his absence'. In the case of articles in the latter form, the alternate is treated for all purposes as if he were a director and in particular details of all such alternates must be registered at Companies House on form 288a. There is no separate form for alternates and no mention of this should be made on the form, although it may be useful to note this in the register of directors. The alternate should be treated for these purposes as a director even if he is never asked to attend a meeting or to serve as a director in his appointor's absence. While an alternate is carrying out the functions of a director, there seems no reason in principle why he should not be subject to the same duties as any other director. However, it is presumably the case that an alternate director is not bound to devote continuous attention to the affairs of the company, if the terms of his appointment are such that he is required only to attend board meetings infrequently or perhaps not at all.

The articles should set out the mechanism by which a director may appoint an alternate; usually this is simply a matter of notifying to the company the identity of a person who has consented to act as an alternate. A person may be a director in his own right and also an alternate for another director. If so, then he may count as two directors for the purposes of the quorum requirement, and his vote will count as two votes. The alternate is the agent of his appointor and the appointor is accordingly able to impose directions on the alternate, as long as these are within the law. In particular, the director can require the alternate to vote in a particular way at the meeting; although whether or not the director would have any remedy in the event of the alternate disregarding these instructions would be a matter of contract law and not a company law matter. In any event, the director could not validly require the alternate to vote in a way which would be contrary to company law.

The appointment of alternates on a regular basis is not appropriate in the case of a company which is to be registered as a charity. The directors of the company will have responsibilities as charity trustees and it would be impossible for an alternate, who will have only an intermittent role in the company, to fulfil those duties. The same principle applies to other directors who have additional legal responsibilities including directors of registered social landlords and insurance companies.

4.4 DIRECTORS' POWERS

4.4.1 Management of the company

Where the members of a company have delegated the authority to manage the company to the board of directors, they do not ordinarily have any power to manage the company themselves. However, if there is no board capable of acting, the members of the company do have certain limited powers to avoid the company reaching a stalemate. For example, the members may appoint additional directors to make a quorate board.[1]

The directors of a company are the company's agents and have such powers as are delegated to them by the articles. The articles will almost always provide for the general management of the company to be in the hands of the directors. Note that the delegation is to the board of directors as a whole[2] and not to individual directors except where the articles (or rules or policies made under them) allow individual delegation, for example to a managing director, finance director and the like. In practice, this rule is often overlooked, but directors should bear in mind when entering any particularly unusual transaction that they should have the authority of the board. However, any act not properly authorised by a unanimous vote of the board members or by a vote properly passed at a board meeting may be 'ratified' or corrected by a resolution at a subsequent board meeting validly convened and held. Approval of the minutes of a previous invalid meeting or resolution can constitute ratification.[3] Any ratifying resolution should itself be recorded carefully in the minutes.

As agents having delegated authority, directors may not themselves delegate their powers unless authorised by the articles. Where delegation is authorised, it will usually be in terms such that the directors are permitted to delegate to committees or to a managing director or both.

4.4.2 Delegation to committees

In a company limited by guarantee, committees may be useful for deliberations on matters such as the admission of new members, setting membership fees, or deciding matters of policy in particular areas. Committees are generally useful for any decisions which may need to be

---

1   *Barron v Potter* [1914] 1 Ch 895.
2   *Re Haycraft Gold Reduction Co* [1900] 2 Ch 230.
3   *Municipal Mutual Insurance Ltd v Harrop* [1998] 2 BCLC 540, ChD.

taken speedily, or which could be the cause of embarrassment to some members of the board.

The articles will normally set out who is eligible for membership of the committees. In some cases, it may be appropriate for the committee to be composed solely of members of the board itself, and this type of committee is easiest to control: the directors of the company remain responsible for the actions of the committee. However, it is possible (and sometimes desirable) for the committee to include some representatives of the company's membership or even outsiders. In order to prevent a loss of control, the board should ensure that clear reporting structures are in place and that the remit of the committee is clearly defined from the start. It would not be advisable for the committee to be able to conduct business if none of the board members were present, and indeed it would arguably have ceased to be a committee of the board at all. As meetings of the committee will be subject to the general law of meetings, it would be sensible for the rules of the committee to include as a safeguard a minimum number of board members as part of the quorum requirement. This type of rule need not be set out in the articles and would be a proper subject for the company's rules or by-laws.[1]

In the case of a registered charity, the Charity Commissioners may be reluctant to allow delegation of all except administrative tasks unless the charity can show good reasons why this is necessary and also that appropriate control mechanisms have been put in place. The Charity Commissioners are particularly concerned to see that the investment powers of the charity trustees are properly used and any delegation of these powers to a committee will be subject to particular scrutiny. The trustees must be able to demonstrate that they remain in overall control of the charity's investments.

4.4.3 Managing director

The articles may permit the appointment of a managing director or other executive to take over the day-to-day running of the company. In the case of a company which is registered as a charity, it is particularly important that any appointment of a managing director should be expressly authorised by the articles. There is a dilemma in the case of a manager of a charity, in that a person who has conduct of the charity's affairs is deemed to be a trustee whether or not he is given that title or appointed as such under the procedure in the constitution. The general principle applied by the Charity Commissioners is that a charity trustee should not be paid. A clause is, therefore, needed in the articles governing the appointment of a manager and authorising payment of a salary.

Where the directors delegate to an employee, not only must the delegation be authorised by the articles but it must also be necessary in the interests of

---

1   See **2.12.7**.

the business. It is also clear that the board of directors cannot, in any event, delegate overall responsibility. In *Re Barings plc (No 5)*,[1] the court was considering the disqualification of three directors in the Barings Bank group who had failed adequately to supervise 'rogue trader' Nick Leeson, whose activities in Singapore led to the collapse of the bank in 1995. There was no question that the directors were not honest, but they had not taken active steps to manage the area of the bank's business in which Leeson was working. In one case, there had been a deliberate 'hands off' policy so that Leeson could carry on his apparently profitable activities without management interference. The court disqualified all three directors, and Jonathan Parker J set out the principles which applied to the duty to supervise. First, all directors had a continuing duty to maintain a sufficient understanding of their company's business to enable them to discharge their duties properly. Secondly, if authorised by the articles, the board of directors were allowed to delegate lower down the management chain, and could place a reasonable degree of trust in the competence and integrity of those to whom they had delegated, but there remained a duty to supervise the delegated functions. Thirdly, the exact extent of this duty to supervise could not be stated as a general principle but would depend on the circumstances of the company and an individual director's responsibility in it.

4.4.4 Authority to bind the company

A director who does not have the power to perform a particular act (for example, to sign a particular contract) is nevertheless likely to be able to bind the company to the contract if he has ostensible authority as an agent of the company. The ostensible authority means the authority usually conferred on a person holding the particular position, or a specific holding out of a person as having a particular authority. A director will normally have ostensible authority unless the person dealing with the company knows that he is not in fact authorised. However, if the director holds himself out as having authority which he does not in fact have, he may be liable to the third party for a breach of warranty of his authority.

In favour of a person dealing with the company in good faith, the power of the board of directors[2] to bind the company, or to authorise others to do so, is deemed to be free of any limitation under the company's constitution.[3] Even knowledge that an act is beyond the directors' powers does not amount to bad faith,[4] and a person is under no duty to enquire (for example, by conducting a search of the company's filing record at Companies House) as to the extent of the directors' authority.[5] However, these provisions are intended to benefit outsiders dealing with the company and do not remove the right of a member of the company to bring an action to restrain the act,

---

1   [1999] 1 BCLC 433.
2   Not an individual director, although he may have ostensible authority.
3   Companies Act 1985, s 35A(1).
4   Companies Act 1985, s 35A(2)(b).
5   Companies Act 1985, s 35B.

except where the act is done in fulfilment of a binding obligation arising from a previous act of the company.[1] If the transaction in excess of the board's powers is a transaction between the company and a director, it is voidable by the company and the director may have to account for the gain made in the transaction,[2] even if he acted in good faith.

The directors' authority rule is modified in the case of companies which are charities, so that it is restricted to commercial arm's length transactions. In the charities legislation,[3] it is provided that ss 35 and 35A of the Companies Act 1985 do not apply to a charity except in favour of a person who either does not know that he deals with a charity, or who does know that he deals with a charity but gives full consideration in money or money's worth and who does not know that the act is not permitted by the memorandum or is beyond the directors' powers, as the case may be. The property rights of a third party without actual knowledge of the breach of the constitution and who pays the full market value for the property are unaffected. Ratification of a breach of the constitution is ineffective without the prior written consent of the Charity Commissioners.

4.5   DIRECTORS' DUTIES

4.5.1   The common law duties

There is no codified statement of directors' duties in the Companies Act 1985. The Law Commission has recommended[4] that there should be a statutory statement of the basic directors' duties, and this has been taken up as a proposal of the Company Law Review.[5] However, there will not be a full codification as it is thought that any codification will be an over-simplification.

There are two sources of common law duties. Directors are placed in a position of trust by the company which appoints them and so have duties as fiduciaries. They are also held to a common law standard of care in performing their functions. In addition, there are statutory duties imposed in the Companies Act 1985 and in other statutes applicable to particular types of companies.

The duties of the directors are primarily owed to the company as a whole and not to an individual member or members, although it is possible that individual members may in some circumstances have a remedy if the

---

1   Companies Act 1985, s 35A(4).
2   Companies Act 1985, s 322A.
3   Charities Act 1993, s 65(1) in England and Wales; Companies Act 1989, s 112(3) for Scotland.
4   *Regulating Conflicts of Interest and Formulating a Statement of Duties* Law Comm 261, Scot Law Comm 173, 22 September 1999.
5   *Developing the Framework: A Consultation Paper from the Steering Group of the Company Law Review*, March 2000 URN 00/656.

directors benefit personally from their breach of duty.[1] Neither are the duties owed to the creditors (except to the extent that remedies available in insolvency proceedings may be for the benefit of creditors, such as ss 213 and 214 of the Insolvency Act 1986). The duties are not owed to employees, and although s 309 of the Companies Act 1985 obliges the directors to have regard to the interests of the employees when they are performing their functions, it expressly provides that the duty is owed to the company as a whole and is enforceable in the same way as any other fiduciary duty. It may be difficult for directors to understand how duties can be owed to what is essentially a legal concept. It may be helpful to analyse the interests of the company as a whole as interests of the current *and future* members.[2]

4.5.2 The duty of skill and care

In the early days of company law, it was thought that there should be no objective standard of behaviour to which directors should aspire. If any question arose as to whether the director had taken sufficient care with the company's business, it was enough to consider whether, taking into account the degree of expertise held by that director, he had come up to the standard which could reasonably be expected of him. In particular, directors were not bound to give continuous attention to the affairs of the company. If they had properly delegated their functions to a manager, or finance director, for example, then they could be held to have discharged their responsibilities.[3] Refusal to attend board meetings so that there was not a quorum would, however, justify the court's intervention.[4]

However, it is now generally accepted that the conduct of a director is required to reach a higher standard. It remains difficult to state what that standard is in any given case, since it is not set out in the Companies Act 1985, and there is always the possibility that an application of the standard in a particular decided case may have been influenced by some peculiarity in the facts. However, it is likely that, even in the case of a company limited by guarantee, a court would apply a standard along the lines of that set out in s 214 of the Insolvency Act 1986. This states that where a company is in insolvent liquidation, the liquidator is entitled to enquire whether or not there has been any wrongful trading by the directors[5] and if there has, the liquidator may apply to the court for a declaration that the director is liable to make a contribution to the company's assets. A director may be guilty of wrongful trading if he has allowed the company to continue trading when he knew or ought to have concluded that there was no reasonable prospect that the company would avoid going into insolvent liquidation. The standard which the court will apply is partly subjective and partly objective,

---

1   *Percival v Wright* [1902] 2 Ch 412; *Peskin and Milner v Andserson and Others* (unreported) 7 December 1999.
2   Megarry J in *Gaiman v National Association for Mental Health* [1971] Ch 317.
3   *Re City Equitable Fire Insurance Co* [1925] Ch 407.
4   *Re Copal Varnish Co Ltd* [1917] 2 Ch 349.
5   Including shadow directors.

being the care which would be taken by a reasonably diligent person having both the skill and experience of that particular director, *and* the skill and experience which may reasonably be expected of a person carrying out the functions of that director in relation to the company.

Since s 214 of the Insolvency Act 1986 looks backward from the insolvent liquidation of a company, there is a strong argument that it provides the standard to which every director should now aspire. The Law Commission has recommended[1] that the dual standard embodied in s 214 should become a statutory definition of the standard of care. Its effect is that, if an amateur takes on a directorship, the standard of care required of him depends upon the functions he carries out in relation to the company but, if an experienced director or manager or a person with a particular skill or qualification (such as a chartered accountant) takes on the job, he will be held to the higher standard which might reasonably be expected of people having that qualification or experience. Directors should note that the court may also make a disqualification order under s 10 of the Company Directors Disqualification Act 1986, if there is a finding of wrongful trading.[2] They may also still be subject to an order made under s 214 relating to their past actions as directors of the company after they have resigned.

In practical terms, the duty of skill and care means that every director must now pay attention to all the affairs of the company. If a director cannot find the time to meet the standard of care required, then he should resign his position. He is entitled to rely on his fellow directors, but should not be slow to challenge information given by them, and should question any signs of misconduct on their part. If he continues to have concerns about some aspect of the company's activities, he should insist that independent advice is taken where appropriate, and he should also make sure that the concerns which he voices at a board meeting are properly recorded in the minutes of that meeting. Having made this formal protest, however, the director should accept the majority's decision, unless he feels that resignation is the only appropriate course of action. Note, however, that a resignation does not absolve the director from all responsibility for actions committed before the resignation.[3] In any event, the existence of s 214 of the Insolvency Act 1986 means that the director should not just allow a situation to continue in the hope that circumstances will improve.

A director is also allowed to rely on advice he obtains from those outside the company, such as the company's solicitors and accountants. Indeed, it may be expected of the director that he should take advice. However, a director cannot absolve himself entirely from responsibility for matters of

---

1   *Regulating Conflicts of Interest and Formulating a Statement of Duties* Law Comm 261, Scot Law Comm 173, 22 September 1999.
2   See Chapter 6.
3   *Industrial Development Consultants Ltd v Cooley* [1972] 1 WLR 443, Birmingham Assize; *Balston Ltd v Headline Filters Ltd* [1990] FSR 385; *Island Export Finance v Umunna* [1986] BCLC 460.

which he should have made himself aware, even if he was in fact ignorant of them.[1]

If the director has concerns that the company may not be able to meet its debts as they fall due, then the director's first duty is to ensure that advice is taken from a licensed insolvency practitioner. The advice may be to put the company into administration; under this procedure, the administrator steps into the shoes of the directors and takes over the management of the company in the interests of the creditors. However, where the company has a loan or overdraft facility where the borrowing is secured by a floating charge over the company's assets, the lender will usually have a veto over the appointment of an administrator, and may wish to appoint an administrative receiver, whose duty is to release sufficient funds to repay the debt.

4.5.3 The duty to act in good faith in the interests of the company

The duty to act in good faith in the interests of the company is the overriding duty of a director and should be borne in mind whenever the director acts. It requires more than honesty: there may be two honest and legal courses of action which a director may take but, in making his choice, he should have regard to the duty to act in the best interests of the company. He should bear in mind that, even if he acts honestly, if there is any misuse of the company's assets, he may be personally liable to compensate the company. The duty has a subjective element: the director must do what he thinks is in the best interests of the company. There is also an objective standard, in that the court will intervene if the director's decision is one which no reasonable director could have reached. If the company has different classes of members then the requirement to act in the best interests of the company means that the director must act fairly between the different classes.

A director must not fetter his discretion as to how to act in the future. He may not, for example, commit himself to defer to someone else's opinion without exercising his own judgement,[2] or put the interests of another employer ahead of those of his company.[3]

4.5.4 The duty to use powers for proper purposes

Even if the director believes that he acts in the best interests of the company, he must not use his powers except for the purposes for which they were given, and must not use them for any collateral purpose. Most of the cases decided on this subject have been about the directors' exercise of their

---

1   *Selangor United Rubber Estates Ltd v Cradock* [1967] 2 All ER 1255.
2   And that other person would become a shadow director: see **4.1.3**.
3   *Scottish Co-operative Wholesale Society Ltd v Meyer* [1959] AC 324, HL.

power to issue shares[1] and so are not particularly useful in the case of most companies limited by guarantee. However, the rule applies where the director uses for his own benefit confidential information or inventions belonging to the company;[2] and where the director takes a commission on a contract negotiated on behalf of the company, even if the company could not itself have benefited from the commission.[3] However, there need not be a personal benefit accruing to the director for a breach of duty to occur, and the principle extends to any use of the company's assets for a purpose which is not permitted by the company's constitution.[4]

4.5.5　Nominee directors

In some companies limited by guarantee, certain directors may be nominated to the board of a company by another organisation, by government, or by a particular group of members. These nominee directors may find that the wishes of their nominating body, or their duties as an employee or director of that nominating body, may conflict with their duties to the company. Company law does not recognise the concept of a nominee director in terms of directors' duties: the director's duty to the company remains paramount,[5] even if this would put him in breach of duty or even in breach of contract with the appointing body. It may, therefore, be necessary for that director to resign from the board if this conflict cannot be resolved.

A related question is whether it is possible for a director also to be a director of a competing company. There is no general prohibition against this,[6] but it is not to be recommended, since it will be very difficult for the director to act in the best interests of both companies at all times. Even if the director is scrupulously careful to avoid favouring one company, there is always the possibility that confidential information belonging to one of the companies will inadvertently be leaked to the other.

4.5.6　Conflict of interests and duty

The general principle is that a director may not put himself into a position where his personal interests conflict with his duties as a director and, in particular, must not vote on a matter in which he is interested, unless the articles specifically authorise his vote. The articles may also restrict whether the director can be counted as part of the quorum. In the absence of such a provision in the articles, the quorum can be made up only of directors who are entitled to vote.

1　Eg *Bamford v Bamford* [1970] Ch 212, CA.
2　*Cranleigh Precision Engineering Ltd v Bryant* [1965] 1 WLR 1293.
3　*Boston Deep Sea Fishing Company v Ansell* (1889) 39 ChD 339.
4　*Re Claridge's Patent Asphalt Co Ltd* [1921] 1 Ch 543.
5　*Scottish Co-operative Wholesale Society v Meyer* [1959] AC 324; *Kuwait Asia Bank EC v National Mutual Life Nominees Ltd* [1991] 1 AC 187, PC.
6　Although there are dicta of Lord Denning in the *Scottish Co-operative* case cited in the previous note to the effect that the nominee rule does prohibit it.

Where a director has a personal interest in a transaction with the company, he has a duty to declare that interest to the board of directors,[1] even if he is the sole director.[2] There are two rules of law behind this principle. One is a principle of equity which requires that directors must make full and frank disclosure of personal transactions, and the transaction must either be specifically authorised by the company in general meeting, or excused by provisions in the articles.[3] Articles of this sort typically cover situations where the interest arises as part of an arrangement made for the benefit of the company such as giving a guarantee or participation in a company pension scheme.

Secondly, however, there is s 317 of the Companies Act 1985 which requires disclosure of the nature of the interest at the meeting of the board of directors at which the question of entering the contract is first taken into consideration, or if the director is not interested in the contract at the date of that meeting, at the next meeting of the directors after he became interested.[4] Section 317 applies whatever is stated in the articles, although it does not require the extent of the interest to be disclosed unless this is required by the articles. If the interest in the contract arises because the director is member of a specified company or firm, the director may make a block disclosure by notice to the directors at a meeting of the directors, relating to contracts made after the date of the notice. Disclosure must be made to a meeting of the board of directors and not to a committee of the board[5] but, if all the directors were informed of the transaction and consented informally, this may be sufficient.[6] Disclosure should be carefully recorded in the minutes of the meeting.

The consequences of breaching these rules are serious. The director who breaches s 317 is liable to a fine. Regardless of whether it is fair that the director should have entered into the contract, it is voidable by the company,[7] unless the company has already affirmed the contract, or there is undue delay before the company seeks to avoid the contract. The contract will also not be voidable if a third party has acquired rights in the subject matter of the contract or it is not possible to restore the original position, for example because the contract concerned property which has been destroyed.

In addition to compliance with s 317 of the Companies Act 1985 and the articles, it may be necessary for there to be an entry in the company's

---

1   *Hutton v West Cork Ry* (1883) 23 ChD 654; *Guinness plc v Saunders*; *Guinness v Ward* [1990] 2 AC 663, HL; [1988] 1 WLR 863, CA.
2   *Neptune (Vehicle Washing Equipment) Ltd v Fitzgerald* [1995] 3 WLR 108, [1995] BCC 474, ChD.
3   Provisions in the articles may not excuse a breach of trust as opposed to preventing a breach of trust arising; see s 310 of the Companies Act 1985 and *Movitex Ltd v Bulfield* [1988] BCLC 104.
4   Companies Act 1985, s 317(2).
5   *Guinness plc v Saunders*; *Guinness v Ward* [1990] 2 AC 663, HL; [1988] 1 WLR 863, CA.
6   *Re Dominion International Group plc (No 2)* [1996] 1 BCLC 572, ChD.
7   *Hely-Hutchinson v Brayhead Ltd* [1968] 1 QB 549, [1967] 3 All ER 98, CA.

register of directors' interests.[1] Every company must have a register of directors' interests, even if it is a company limited by guarantee without a share capital. The reason is that s 324 of the Companies Act 1985, which requires the director to disclose certain interests, relates not only to shares in the company itself but also to shares in certain companies in the same group, and to interests in the company's debentures.

Note that there are provisions of the Insolvency Act 1986 which enable the liquidator[2] of a company to look back at contracts concluded by the company in the period leading up to the liquidation and in some circumstances to unravel those contracts. Certain transactions concluded at an undervalue (ie at less than market value) in the two years preceding the liquidation may be set aside by the court on the application of the liquidator.[3] The liquidator may also apply to the court to set aside a transaction that constitutes a preference by the company in favour of any creditor;[4] in other words, if the effect of the transaction would be to put the creditor in a better position in the event of liquidation than would otherwise have been the case. In the case of a transaction with a connected person (including a director or a member of his family) then the relevant period before the liquidation is two years, and the transaction is presumed to be an unfair preference unless the contrary is proved.

4.5.7   Personal profits

A director must account to the company for any personal profit made from his office other than the remuneration and other benefits properly authorised by the articles or by the company in general meeting. This is the case even if the company itself could not have benefited from the transaction.[5]

However, the company's members may, by passing an ordinary resolution, ratify the secret profit once they have become fully aware of the relevant facts and provided that the votes of the director in question are not needed in order to pass the resolution.[6]

A director has, therefore, no right to remuneration (including pension) for his office unless this is authorised by the articles or a resolution of the members.[7] Regulation 82 of Table A to the Companies Act 1985, which may be adopted in some companies limited by guarantee, requires the authorisation of the director's remuneration by the company in general meeting. It may be better to follow the practice of most companies and to have the director's pay determined by his fellow directors or by a

---

1   Companies Act 1985, s 325.
2   Or administrator.
3   Insolvency Act 1986, s 238.
4   Insolvency Act 1986, s 239.
5   *Regal (Hastings) Ltd v Gulliver* [1942] 1 All ER 378.
6   *Cook v Deeks* [1916] 1 AC 554.
7   *Re George Newman & Co* [1895] 1 Ch 674.

remuneration committee. If the payment of remuneration is proper, then it amounts to a debt owed by the company and the director may enforce it as a debt.[1] Unless the articles or the company in general meeting specifically authorise the payment of expenses in addition to the standard remuneration, the remuneration is taken to cover the directors' expenses.[2]

In a charity, the directors of the company will also be the charity trustees and the general principle is that a trustee should not profit from his trust, although the reimbursement of expenses will not contravene this rule. The Charity Commissioners will look very closely at any provision in the company's memorandum and articles which permits the payment of salary or fees to directors and will accept payment provisions only in very exceptional circumstances where the payments can be justified as in the best interests of the charity and necessary for its effective administration.

4.5.8 Ratification by the company in general meeting

If an act in excess of the directors' powers is not unlawful or ultra vires, it may be ratified by the members of the company, either by an ordinary resolution passed at a properly convened meeting or by unanimous approval of the members by a written resolution,[3] provided the company is not insolvent. The director may vote in the matter unless there is dishonesty on the part of the director or where the effect of the resolution would be to authorise a benefit accruing to the director and not to the company.

If the articles or general company law require a special procedure to be followed which has not been followed, the ratification of the directors' act must be by unanimous resolution of the members even where ratification is proposed at a meeting. If the act is unlawful or ultra vires, it may be ratified by a special resolution passed at a meeting or by unanimous approval of the members not at a meeting. However, a separate special resolution or unanimous approval will be required in order to relieve the directors of liability.

4.5.9 Remedies for a breach of the directors' duties

The company may obtain damages from the directors who participated in the wrongful act on a joint and several basis, or, in appropriate cases, it may be able to obtain an injunction to restrain the breach. Restoration of the property or an account of profits made by the director may also be ordered. The company may bring an action for negligence, breach of trust or breach of duty up to six years after the alleged act, but there is no limitation defence (ie that the claim has been brought too late) available to the director if there is fraud or the wrongful receipt of the company's property.

---

1   *Nell v Atlanta Gold etc Mines* (1895) 11 TLR 407.
2   *Young v Naval and Military Co-op Society* [1905] 1 KB 687.
3   *Grant v United Kingdom Switchback Railway Co* (1888) 40 ChD 135.

It follows from the principle that the duties of directors are primarily owed to the company as a whole, that if there is a wrong done to the company, then an individual member or a minority of members should not be able to sue the director or directors in question. If the member does not wish to propose that the company should be wound up because this would be just and equitable, the member does have a potential remedy under s 459 of the Companies Act 1985, where the company's affairs have been conducted in a manner unfairly prejudicial to his interests *as a member*. In a case concerning a company limited by guarantee set up as a workers' co-operative, the judge struck out as an abuse of process a petition under s 459 alleging that a member's dismissal as an employee and as a director was unfairly prejudicial, on the grounds that it was not prejudicial to his interests as a member.[1]

Unfairly prejudicial conduct does not necessarily entail discrimination between different members or different classes of member. It can be conduct which is unfairly prejudicial to the members as a whole. Examples would be a failure to hold annual general meetings or to present accounts to the members; the misappropriation of assets; or alterations to the articles which are not in the interests of the company as a whole.[2] The court has wide powers to remedy the unfair prejudice, including the power to alter the memorandum or articles.

The House of Lords in the important case of *O'Neill v Phillips*[3] has restricted the use of s 459 petitions. 'Fairness' in s 459 was held to be related to the rules for the conduct of the company to which the members had agreed (the articles, by-laws and any extrinsic contracts) and to the equitable concept of good faith, derived from the law of partnership. A member can complain of unfairness only if there is a breach of the rules or if the rules are applied in a manner contrary to the requirement of good faith.

Almost all s 459 petitions have concerned companies limited by shares owned and managed by a small group of people. These cases have been particularly expensive and time-consuming; the parties have to fund the litigation themselves as the company's funds cannot be used for this purpose. However, the Civil Procedure Rules 1998 (the implementation of the Woolf reforms) have increased the case management role of judges, and encouraged the use of mediation as an alternative to court proceedings. It is hoped that these new Rules will speed up the process and avoid wasted costs.

4.5.10   Companies with particular status

Directors of charitable companies are also charity trustees and are also subject to duties under charity law. The duties of charity trustees are

---

1   *Re Alchemea Ltd* [1998] BCC 964, ChD.
2   *Greenhalgh v Arderne Cinemas* [1920] 2 All ER 1120.
3   [1999] 1 WLR 1092, HL.

helpfully set out in Charity Commission publications available free from their offices or their web site.[1] They include duties to secure the proper and effective use of the charity's property, and to invest the funds not immediately required for use in furtherance of the charity's purposes.

Directors of insurance companies are also obliged to conduct the business of their companies in accordance with the criteria of sound and prudent management set out in Sch 2 to the Insurance Companies Act 1982. These include criteria relating to the skill of individual directors, the keeping of books and records, and compliance with the law.

The Housing Corporation has the power to appoint or to remove the directors of registered social landlords. In addition to the company law duties, directors of these companies must comply with the performance management standards laid down by the Housing Corporation.

4.6 STATUTORY PROVISIONS RELATING TO DIRECTORS

4.6.1 Service contracts

Copies of all directors'[2] service contracts[3] which have more than a year left to run must be kept at 'an appropriate place' which generally means the registered office or principal place of business[4] of the company. If a director's service contract is not kept at the registered office, then a form must be filed at Companies House notifying the address at which the contract is kept.[5] The copy contracts must be available for inspection by members of the company without charge.[6]

It is rarely in the interests of a company to bind itself to excessively long terms of service for a director. Section 319 of the Companies Act 1985 applies to both service (employment) contracts and to contracts for services (usually called consultancy contracts).[7] It requires approval by a resolution of the company in general meeting of a term in a contract with a director such that the director's employment may continue for a period of more than five years, during which the employment cannot be terminated by the company by notice, or when the company's right to terminate is limited to particular circumstances. The contracts governed by s 319 include fixed-term contracts and contracts in which the period of service is extendable by

---

1   http://www.charity-commission.gov.uk/.
2   And service contracts with shadow directors: Companies Act 1985, s 318(6).
3   Or, if the contract is not in writing, a memorandum of its terms: Companies Act 1985, s 318(1)(b). Variations of contracts are treated as contracts: Companies Act 1985, s 318(10).
4   See Companies Act 1985, s 318(3).
5   Companies Act 1985, s 318(4).
6   There are criminal penalties for breach of s 218: see Companies Act 1985, s 318(8).
7   Companies Act 1985, s 319(7)(a).

the director to a period of more than five years. There are restrictions on devices designed to circumvent s 319, by executing a contract for a period of less than five years and then agreeing a new contract for a similar period before the end of the first contract.[1] If there is a breach of s 319, the term in question is void and the contract is deemed to include a term entitling the company to terminate the contract on reasonable notice.[2]

The Companies Act 1985 requires that there should be a written memorandum of the terms of the contract made available at the company's registered office for not less than 15 days ending with the date of the meeting at which the resolution approving the contract is to be proposed; and at the meeting itself. Section 319 suggests that a meeting is always required, although it has been held that unanimous consent of the members of the company will suffice.[3] In the case of a charity, the Charity Commisioners' consent will also be required.[4]

4.6.2   Loans to directors

Detailed rules contained in ss 330 to 342 of the Companies Act 1985 restrict loans which may validly be made to directors. Straightforward cash loans to a director of less than £5,000 in aggregate are permitted.[5] It is unlikely that many companies limited by guarantee will have the resources to make loans exceeding this amount to directors; those which do may be prohibited from providing benefits of this sort to directors and so a detailed examination of the rules is beyond the scope of this book. The rules are the same in companies limited by guarantee as they are in companies limited by shares and so readers should consult any of the major company law textbooks. In summary, there are restrictions on the following types of transaction.

(1)   Loans and guarantees for loans provided by third parties, except for certain loans to provide the director with funds to perform his duties.[6]
(2)   The repayment of a director's creditor (a quasi-loan) subject to similar qualifications.[7]
(3)   Hire purchase and other credit transactions benefiting directors.[8]
(4)   Back-to-back loan transactions with third parties, including arrangements within a group of companies.[9]

---

1   Companies Act 1985, s 319(2).
2   Companies Act 1985, s 319(6).
3   *Wright v Atlas Wright (Europe) Ltd*, (1999) *The Times*, February 3, CA; *Re R W Peak (King's Lynn) Ltd* [1998] 1 BCLC 193, ChD.
4   Charities Act 1993, s 66.
5   Companies Act 1985, s 334.
6   Companies Act 1985, ss 330(2), 334 and 337; and see Charities Act 1993, s 66.
7   Companies Act 1985, ss 331(3) and 332.
8   Companies Act 1985, ss 331(7), 330(4), 325 and 337.
9   Companies Act 1985, ss 330(7) and 336.

There are both civil[1] and criminal[2] sanctions for breaches of the provisions. Loans to directors also have particular tax consequences for the company and for the director.

4.6.3 Property transactions involving directors

Section 320 of the Companies Act 1985 requires the prior approval of an ordinary resolution of the company in general meeting for transactions in which a director (or shadow director) acquires from the company, or the company acquires from the director, 'non-cash assets' above a certain value. The section extends to directors of the company's holding company and to persons 'connected with'[3] the director. It applies to any type of asset other than cash,[4] of which the value is not less than £2,000 and is more than the lower of £100,000 or 10 per cent of the company's asset value. The asset value is determined by reference to the accounts for the last financial year in respect of which accounts were prepared. If no accounts have been prepared, the asset value is equal to the called-up share capital. This immediately gives a problem in the case of a company limited by guarantee without a share capital, if the transaction takes place before the first accounts are prepared. Transactions with directors are perhaps more likely to occur in the start up phase. It is recommended, therefore, that in those circumstances, the company should obtain the members' approval to all property transactions with directors where the value of the asset is £2,000 or more. It was, however, held by the court in the case of a company limited by shares that it was for the person alleging that the value exceeded the relevant limit to prove this was the case.[5]

There are some limited exceptions in s 321. In the case of a company limited by guarantee, the exception which might seem to be most helpful is where an asset is acquired by the director in his capacity as member of the company. This exception is given no further explanation and it should be used with caution, as it may not be clear in what capacity the director is dealing in the asset. It does not apply where the company acquires an asset from the director, and so is of no use, for example, where a company takes an asset from a director in lieu of a subscription or a membership fee. Section 320 of the Companies Act 1985 will apply to this transaction if the asset's value is within the financial limits.

If the company does not comply with s 320, the transaction is voidable at the instance of the company, except in the circumstances set out in s 322 of the Companies Act 1985. Whether or not the transaction has already been avoided by the company, if there is a breach of s 320, the director (and any

---

1   Companies Act 1985, s 341.
2   Companies Act 1985, s 342.
3   See s 346 of the Companies Act 1985.
4   'Non-cash assets' is interpreted in accordance with s 739 of the Companies Act 1985 to include interests in property.
5   *Joint Receivers and Managers of Niltan Carson Ltd v Hawthorne* [1988] BCLC 298.

person connected with him) and any other director who authorised the transaction are jointly liable to indemnify the company against all losses which it has suffered as a result of the contravention of s 320 and to account for any personal gain they have made. The breach of s 320 is regarded as a misapplication of the company's assets and the director is required to restore the full value to the company. This means that if the diminution in the value of the asset since the appropriation is partly due to a declining market price the director is still liable to compensate the company for the full amount of the loss.[1] If the director has attached a special value to the asset above the market value then he is liable to compensate the company by reference to that higher, subjective value.[2]

4.6.4 Accounts

One of the duties which is most rigorously enforced by the law is the duty of a company to keep proper accounts and to make the appropriate annual accounts and reports. Failure to comply with the requirements set out below will in most cases make the directors liable to punishment by a fine or in some cases imprisonment.

The duties to keep accounting records are set out in ss 221 to 222. The accounting records must be sufficient to show and explain the company's transactions; to disclose, with reasonable accuracy, the company's current financial position; and to enable the directors to prepare the profit and loss account and balance sheet (required by s 226). The records must be kept at the registered office or such other place as the directors think fit, and must be available for inspection by the company's officers. The records must be kept for a period of three years, although in practice all companies must keep their records for at least six years since as part of an investigation the Inland Revenue may make assessments for up to six previous years, or for up to 20 previous years if there is evidence of fraudulent or negligent conduct.

The directors remain primarily responsible for drawing up the annual accounts even if they engage an accountant to do this on their behalf. The detailed requirements as to the content of the accounts and the accompanying directors' report are beyond the scope of this work, but note that in many cases a company limited by guarantee will be able to take advantage of many exemptions available to small and medium-sized companies. In particular, a small company[3] which is not also a charity with a balance sheet total of less than £1.4 million and an annual turnover below £1 million[4] is not obliged to have its accounts audited. Any company which is not able to take advantage of this exemption or the exemption for dormant companies (see s 250 of the Companies Act 1985) will be required to have its accounts

---

1   *Re Duckwari plc (No 2)* [1998] 3 WLR 913, CA.
2   *Micro Leisure Ltd v County Properties and Developments Ltd* (2000) *The Times,* January 12 (Scottish Court of Session on a motion to amend pleadings).
3   As defined by s 246 of the Companies Act 1985.
4   Companies Act 1985 (Audit Exemption) (Amendment) Regulations 2000, SI 2000/1430.

audited. This includes, for example, insurance companies and, in most cases, parent and subsidiary companies. The accounts will accordingly be required to be accompanied by an auditor's report. Not less than 10 per cent in number of the company's members may require the accounts for a particular financial year to be audited, by depositing a notice in writing at the registered office of the company not less than one month before the end of the financial year in question.

In the case of a company which is a charity, different conditions apply; the company may not need an audit if its balance sheet total does not exceed £1.4 million, and it may submit to the Charity Commissioners a report prepared by a 'reporting accountant' if its gross income does not exceed £250,000; or no report at all, if its gross income does not exceed £90,000 (unless the company is a parent or subsidiary or at least 10 per cent of its membership votes for an audit).

4.6.5 Laying accounts and reports before the company

Most companies will be obliged to lay accounts and reports before the company in general meeting[1] within a period of 10 months after the end of the company's financial year.[2] However, if all the members of the company agree, the company may pass an elective resolution[3] to remove this requirement,[4] subject to a power given to any member to require the accounts and reports to be laid before the company in general meeting.[5] If the elective resolution is passed it does not, however, remove the requirement to send out the accounts to the members within the 10-month period; the accounts and reports must be sent out not less than 28 days before the end of the 10-month period[6] and they must be accompanied by a statement reminding the member of his right to have the accounts laid before a general meeting. In any event, any member of a company, whether or not the elective resolution has been passed, has the right to demand copies of the company's last annual accounts at any time.[7]

4.6.6 Filing accounts and reports at Companies House

The company must deliver the accounts and reports required to Companies House within 10 months after the end of the accounting period of the company. This is a strict limit and Companies House will fine the company if the accounts are even one day late. The penalties for late filing start at £100 and rise on a sliding scale to £1,000 depending on the length of the default. In exceptional circumstances, Companies House may allow the accounts to be filed outside the strict time-limit but only if a written,

---

1   Companies Act 1985, s 241.
2   Companies Act 1985, s 244(1).
3   See **5.5.4**.
4   Companies Act 1985, s 252.
5   Companies Act 1985, s 253(2).
6   Companies Act 1985, s 253(1).
7   Companies Act 1985, s 239.

reasoned application has been made on behalf of the company within the time limit. This power is discretionary and is exercised only where the delay is unavoidable, for example if one of the directors dies, and not just because (for example) the company's accountants are exceptionally busy. In an order proposed under the Electronic Communications Bill, it is proposed that companies should be able to send accounts to the members electronically (including by posting them on a web site).[1]

4.6.7 Signatures

The balance sheet should be signed by a director and a director or the secretary should sign the directors' report. The copy bearing the original signatures should be filed at Companies House and this copy must also comply with the registrar of companies' detailed requirements as to document quality.[2]

4.7 REMOVAL OF A DIRECTOR BY THE MEMBERS OF THE COMPANY

4.7.1 Resolution to remove director

Section 303 of the Companies Act 1985 provides that a director may be removed by an ordinary resolution of which 'special notice' has been given. This applies even if the director is appointed in the articles as 'life director', or if removal would breach the terms of a contract with the director, although the Act does not remove the right of the director to be compensated in accordance with the contract.[3] Special notice[4] means that the person proposing that the director should be removed must have given to the company not less than 28 days' notice of the intention to move the resolution, before the meeting at which it is to be moved. The company must then give the members notice of the resolution at the same time as the notice of meeting is sent out. If that is not practicable, it may give notice of the resolution by a newspaper advertisement or by any other method allowed by the company's articles at least 21 days before the meeting. Failure to give the required notice of the meeting does not mean that the meeting has been invalidly called.

The resolution removing a director does not need to give the reasons for removal, but the director has the right to be notified of the proposal to remove him as a director and to be heard at the meeting at which the resolution is to be proposed. He also has the right to make written representations to the company of a reasonable length. If these represen-

---

1   *Electronic Communications for Companies: An Order Under the Electronic Communications Bill (A Consultative Document)* February 2000 URN 00/626.
2   See www.companieshouse.gov.uk.
3   Companies Act 1985, s 303(5).
4   Companies Act 1985, s 379.

tations are received by the company in time, they must be sent out with the notices convening the meeting. If they arrive too late and the notices have already been sent out, or if the company does not comply with the rule requiring circulation, then the director has the right to have them read out at the meeting. The company need not circulate the representations if it[1] applies to the court on the grounds that the rights under s 303 are being used to secure needless publicity for defamatory matter.

Section 303 of the Companies Act 1985 provides a mechanism for removing a director which cannot be overridden by the articles. However, the articles can and should provide for the office of director to be vacated in other circumstances, such as bankruptcy, mental incapacity, or prohibition by law.[2] The articles may provide for the board to be able to remove one of their fellow board members. This power is given to the directors in a fiduciary capacity and so must be exercised in the best interests of the company as a whole. The articles may provide for the office of director to be vacated if the holder's contract of employment is terminated. Without the provision in the articles, it would be necessary for the company to go through the procedure in s 303 in addition to whatever steps are required by the employment contract.

A director cannot prevent his removal in his capacity as a director but, if he is also a member of the company, he may have weighted voting rights on a resolution to remove him.[3] Orders made under s 459 of the Companies Act 1985 now also extend to protecting the legitimate interest of a member of a small company to be a member of the board, even though there is no contractual right as a member to be elected to the board.[4]

4.7.2   Unfair dismissal

The dismissal of the director under s 303 may be a breach of the director's employment contract, unless the contract can be performed without the employee having a place on the board of directors. This would apply for example where the director was described as the company accountant. The articles do not constitute a contract with the director in that capacity although they may in some cases be evidence of its terms. The Companies Act 1985[5] provides that payments to a director in compensation for loss of office[6] or in consideration of or in connection with his retirement from office are to be disclosed to the members of the company in advance and approved by an ordinary resolution or unanimous written resolution.

---

1   Or any other person aggrieved: Companies Act 1985, s 304(4).
2   Such as under the Company Directors Disqualification Act 1986 or the Charities Act 1993.
3   *Bushell v Faith* [1970] AC 1099, [1970] 2 WLR 272, [1970] 1 All ER 53, although it is sometimes said that the ratio of this case extends only to quasi partnership companies.
4   *O'Neil v Phillips* [1999] 1 WLR 1092, HL.
5   Companies Act 1985, s 312.
6   But not damages for breach of contract or payments by way of pension in respect of past services: Companies Act 1985, s 316(3).

After one year of service, an employee has the right under the Employment Rights Act 1996 not to be unfairly dismissed, and to claim compensation if he is unfairly dismissed. The fact that the company may have complied with the provisions of s 303 does not mean that the company has satisfied the burden that is placed upon it to show that the dismissal of the director is fair. Nothing in the articles of association of the employer company has any effect on the statutory rights given to an employee to protect him against unfair dismissal. The dismissal may be fair if it was for redundancy, misconduct, incapability (including ill-health), illegality, or some other substantial reason, and if the employer has acted reasonably and has followed a fair procedure for the dismissal. The maximum compensatory award was increased in 1999 to £50,000. In cases of sex discrimination, race discrimination and discrimination on grounds of disability, there is no limit on the compensatory award. There is also no limit if the employee is dismissed for 'whistleblowing' or for complaining about a breach of health and safety rules.

4.8 PERSONAL LIABILITY

4.8.1 Civil liability

A director may be made personally responsible for the company's debts in certain circumstances. Section 349 of the Companies Act 1985 makes a director who signs certain instruments such as a cheque or order for goods or services personally liable to the creditor if the company's full name[1] does not appear on the instrument and the company does not pay the sum due.

The director may be jointly liable with the company for torts[2] (civil wrongs, including negligence) committed by the company if he was actively involved in the wrong or if he directed that the wrong should be done.[3] The mere fact that he is a director at the material time does not suffice, but he may be personally liable when he ordered or procured the acts of other persons which render the company liable,[4] or if he personally assumed responsibility for the company's actions.[5] If a director is found to be jointly liable, the director and the company face the full amount of the liability being imposed upon them, and judgment against one of them does not bar an action against the other.[6]

---

1   Limited may be shortened to ltd.
2   Under English law.
3   *T Oertli AG v E J Bowman (London) Ltd and Ors* [1956] RPC 282.
4   *C Evans & Son Ltd v Spritebrand Ltd* [1985] 1 WLR 317, [1985] 2 All ER 415; *Standard Chartered Bank v Pakistan National Shipping Corporation and Another* [1999] 1 All ER Comm 417, (1999) *The Independent*, 9 December, CA.
5   *Williams v Natural Life Health Foods* [1998] 2 All ER 577, HL.
6   Civil Liability (Contribution) Act 1978, s 3.

The director may also be made personally liable in certain circumstances if the company is wound up, under provisions of the Insolvency Act 1986.[1] Section 214 of the 1986 Act[2] applies if the company is insolvent; but s 213 of the Insolvency Act 1986 applies whether or not the company is insolvent. Section 213 allows the liquidator to apply to the court for an order which any person (whether or not a director of the company) who was knowingly a party to carrying on the company's business with the intent to defraud creditors of the company or for any other fraudulent purpose should be required to contribute to the company's assets. A director of a company which uses the name of a former company of which he was a director and which was put into insolvent liquidation, may be made liable for the debts of the new company.[3]

4.8.2 Crimes

Certain provisions of the Companies Act 1985 impose criminal penalties on directors. The typical form of those penalties is that a director commits an offence under the Act if he has knowingly and wilfully authorised or permitted the default.[4] The penalty will depend upon the court in which the director is convicted: in a magistrates' court the maximum term of imprisonment is six months. In some cases the fines are limited by reference to the 'standard scale'. At the time of writing the maximum fine on this scale is £5,000.

4.8.3 Indemnity and relief by the court

Where a director is pursued by the company for negligence, breach of trust or breach of duty, or where criminal penalties are imposed for breaches of the Companies Act 1985 and related legislation, a director who has acted honestly and reasonably may be excused by the court under s 727 of the Companies Act 1985. It is also possible for a director to use s 727 in anticipation of a claim being made against him.[5] The articles of the company may excuse the director's conduct, although s 310 of the Companies Act 1985 may apply to invalidate or to limit the scope of an article.[6]

---

1 And see also **4.5.6** on setting aside certain transactions with a director.
2 See **4.5.2**.
3 Insolvency Act 1986, s 217.
4 Section 730 of and Sch 24 to the Companies Act 1985 govern the imposition of criminal penalties for breaches of the Act.
5 Companies Act 1985, s 727(2).
6 See **2.12.6**.

4.9 DISQUALIFICATION OF DIRECTORS

A director may be disqualified by the court under the Company Directors Disqualification Act 1986.[1] This Act sets out the various circumstances in which a disqualification order may be made.

(1) On conviction of an indictable offence (s 2).
(2) For persistent default in complying with the companies legislation (s 3) or on summary conviction for a filing or notice default under the Companies Act 1985 (s 5).
(3) For fraud committed in the winding up of a company (s 4).
(4) Following an investigation into the company's affairs by the Department of Trade and Industry (s 8) or an application under ss 213 or 214 of the Insolvency Act 1986 (s 10).

If the court finds that a person is unfit to serve as a director, it is *obliged* to disqualify the director for a minimum of two years. Schedule 1 to the Company Directors Disqualification Act 1986 sets out the circumstances which may lead to a finding of unfitness. The Schedule is divided into Part I, which applies in all cases, and Part II, which applies where the company is insolvent.

The court will balance the need to protect the public from unfit directors and the aim of not discouraging entrepreneurial spirit. In *Re Deaduck Ltd, Baker v Secretary of State for Trade and Industry*,[2] the court held that it would put directors 'in an unfair and unrealistic position ... if every time a director was found to have failed in his duty, he was liable to be disqualified'. In that case, the court reduced a period of disqualification (for making a payment which was detrimental to the company's creditors) because the director had not been 'guilty of dishonest or commercially flagrantly culpable behaviour', and because he had not been given the chance at the original hearing to deal with certain allegations. However, the fact that the director has not been dishonest is not the deciding factor in every case, and the court will take a broad look at the director's responsibilities in each case.[3]

In addition, a director of a company which is a registered social landlord may be liable to be disqualified under provisions in the Housing Act 1996.[4]

---

1   Proceedings under the Act are civil proceedings and not criminal proceedings; evidence given in Insolvency Act proceedings may be used in support of the case for disqualification without breaching the directors' human rights: *Re Westminster Property Management Ltd* (2000) *The Times*, January 19.
2   [1999] All ER (D) 562.
3   *Re Barings Plc (No 5)* [1999] 1 BCLC 433, CA.
4   Schedule 1, paras 25, 26.

Chapter 5

COMPANY MEETINGS

5.1 MEETINGS OF THE MEMBERS OF THE COMPANY

5.1.1 The requirement to hold meetings

Meetings of the members of the company are required by many provisions of the Companies Act 1985. In addition, the articles of a company may require a meeting of the members to be held for a particular purpose, such as the admission of a member.[1] Unless the articles provide otherwise, the members of a company may effect any decision which may be made by a company by passing an ordinary resolution.[2] However, almost all companies will make the directors agents of the company for the majority of purposes by means of an express provision of the articles. For example, see Appendix A; or Table A, reg 70 (which is not excluded, in the case of companies limited by guarantee, by Table C) which provides as follows:

> '**70**. Subject to the provisions of the Acts, the memorandum and the articles and to any directions given by special resolution, the business of the company shall be managed by the directors who may exercise all the powers of the company. No alteration of the memorandum or articles and no such direction shall invalidate any prior act of the directors which would have been valid if that alteration had not been made or that direction had not been given. The powers given by this regulation shall not be limited by any special power given to the directors by the articles and a meeting of directors at which a quorum is present may exercise all powers exercisable by the directors.'

Where there is a provision which gives the directors day-to-day control over the running of the company, the power to make decisions by ordinary resolution reverts to the members only when the directors waive their authority, or where they are incapable of acting owing to the fact that the board meeting is inquorate, deadlocked, or where a vote cannot be taken owing to directors' conflict of interests.[3]

Meetings of classes of members may also be required,[4] as may meetings of debenture holders. It should be noted that the convenors of a meeting cannot transform one type of meeting into another simply because the same people are required to be present at each. For example, a directors' meeting

---

1   See **3.2**.
2   See **5.5.1**.
3   *Barron v Potter* [1914] 1 Ch 895.
4   For example, for s 425 schemes of arrangement: see **6.8**.

cannot turn into a members' meeting even if all the members are also directors. However, in those circumstances the members could agree, in their capacity as members, to the calling of the meeting at short notice,[1] or they might be able to deal with the matters for the general meeting by means of a written resolution.[2]

5.1.2   Annual general meeting

A company must hold an annual general meeting (AGM) every year unless it has passed an elective resolution.[3] The notice of meeting must state that the meeting is the AGM.[4] The only exception is that in the year of incorporation and the following year there need not be an AGM, provided that there is an AGM within 18 months of incorporation. The interval between each AGM must not be greater than 15 months. This is to avoid abuse of the requirement to hold annual meetings by holding one AGM in January of calendar year one and the next in December of calendar year two. The provisions of the Companies Act 1985 relating to AGMs are reinforced by criminal sanctions which may attach to the company and its officers.

It is usual for an AGM to be held soon after the annual accounts of the company are prepared, although the rules relating to the delivery of accounts to Companies House and the completion of an Inland Revenue return are not currently linked to the provisions of the Companies Act 1985 relating to the holding of the AGM. One of the proposals in the Company Law Review is that there should be such a link, which would mean delaying the date of a company's first AGM. The Review also contains a proposal to remove the requirement for small private companies to have an AGM. The reasoning behind this proposal is that the AGM is the mechanism by which the members hold the management to account and this is most essential in the case of larger companies, and particularly in the case of listed companies. It may, however, be the case that an AGM will continue to be required for a company limited by guarantee with a large membership. It is also possible that companies limited by guarantee may be overlooked entirely in this part of the Review.

5.1.3   Elective regime

The Companies Act 1989 inserted provisions permitting a company to dispense with the holding of an AGM by passing an elective resolution under the Companies Act 1985.[5] These provisions apply even if the requirement to hold an AGM is also contained in the articles.[6] The elective

---

1   See **5.2.1**.
2   See **5.5.5**.
3   See **5.5.4**.
4   Companies Act 1985, s 366.
5   Companies Act 1985, s 366A.
6   Companies Act 1985, s 379A(5).

resolution will have effect in the year in which it is made and in subsequent years, unless and until either the company passes an ordinary resolution revoking the elective resolution;[1] or the resolution's effect is suspended for a particular year by a member of the company requiring an AGM. This must be done by notice to the company given not later than three months before the end of the year.[2] If the resolution is revoked, the company is not obliged to call an AGM if there are fewer than three months left of the year in which the resolution is passed.[3]

5.1.4 Extraordinary general meetings and members' requisitions

Any general meeting of the company which is not an AGM is an extraordinary general meeting (EGM). The articles will usually set out who may call an EGM but, in addition to the usual power to call meetings conferred on the secretary or the board or both, the Companies Act 1985 provides that members are able to insist on a meeting being called whatever is said in the articles.[4] In the case of a company limited by guarantee, a meeting may be requisitioned by members representing not less than one-tenth of the total voting rights of all the members having a right to vote at general meetings.[5] The relevant date for determining the voting rights is the date on which the requisition is deposited at the registered office of the company. The requisition must state the objects of the meeting and must be signed by all the requisitionists, although not necessarily on the same piece of paper. The directors must call a meeting 'forthwith'[6] and in any event within 21 days, to be held on a date not later than 28 days after the date of the notice. In other words the latest date for a meeting to be held is seven weeks after the requisition.[7] If the directors fail to meet either of these deadlines, the requisitionists (or any of them representing more than one half of the total voting rights of all of them) may call a meeting themselves. This meeting must not be more than three months after the date of deposit of the requisition. The Companies Act 1985 rules relating to the giving of notice, and any supplementary rules in the articles, must be followed by the requisitionists. The company must pay the reasonable expenses of the requisitionists and must deduct them from the fees or salary of the directors who were in default.[8]

The rules relating to members' requisitions of meetings were considered in one of the cases arising out of the re-organisation of the Royal Automobile

---

1   Companies Act 1985, s 379A(3).
2   Companies Act 1985, s 366A(3).
3   Companies Act 1985, s 366A(5).
4   Companies Act 1985, s 368.
5   Companies Act 1985, s 368(2)(b).
6   Companies Act 1985, s 368(1).
7   The Company Law Review proposes to retain the substance of this, but the time-limits may change.
8   Companies Act 1985, s 368(6).

Club, a group of companies including companies limited by guarantee.[1] The members' requisitions had been properly made and deposited, but before a meeting was called pursuant to the requisition, the board called an EGM of its own accord. It was held that the requisitioned meeting should still be called. However, on the facts, the resolutions proposed to be considered at the meeting were invalid, and the court held that as a matter of commercial common sense, if an EGM called pursuant to the requisitions could only be for the purposes of passing ineffective resolutions, the directors need not call the EGM.

These rules relating to the members' requisitions apply whatever is stated in the articles. Therefore, unless it is intended to give a right to call a meeting to members representing less than one-tenth of the total voting rights, it is preferable in the interests of simplicity to omit any express provisions from the articles relating to requisitions. If it is desired to reduce the required level of voting rights, the best way of doing this is to refer to s 368(2)(b) and provide for a figure to be substituted for the one-tenth figure stated there.

5.2   NOTICE OF MEMBERS' MEETINGS

5.2.1   Length of notice for calling meetings

Articles will usually set out in full the rules which apply to the calling of meetings even though many of these rules are found in the Companies Act 1985 because it is more convenient for the company's officers to have a single source of reference for the applicable rules. This also allows the company's members to see that the company has been properly administered. However, many of the provisions of the Act are mandatory and criminal penalties attach to their breach. The amount of notice required will depend on the types of resolution to be proposed at the meeting, the type of the meeting, and any special provisions of the articles. The following principles apply: an AGM or an EGM at which a special resolution is to be proposed must be called by at giving at least 21 days' written notice; and any other meeting must be called by at least 14 days' written notice. The articles may provide for a longer notice period but not for a shorter one.[2] The term 'special notice' as used in the Companies Act 1985 has a specific meaning which will affect the time when notices have to be sent out.[3]

An AGM may be called at short notice if agreed by all the members entitled to attend and vote at it. An EGM, even an EGM at which a special resolution is to be proposed, may be called at short notice if agreed by the 'requisite majority'. The 'requisite majority' is members holding not less than 95 per cent of the total voting rights exercisable at that meeting, unless an elective resolution has been passed which reduces the requisite majority.

---

1   *Rose v McGivern & Ors* [1998] 2 BCLC 593, ChD.
2   Companies Act 1985, s 369(1).
3   See **4.7**.

The smallest majority that can be prescribed is 90 per cent. The rules permitting the calling of a meeting at short notice do not remove the need to issue a notice in the correct form, although the meeting can be called informally and the formal notice document, together with a form of consent to short notice for signature, can be handed out at the meeting itself.

No notice need be given of an adjourned meeting unless this is required by the articles.[1] If the articles require notice to be given but do not specify a period of notice, then the same period of notice should be allowed as was required for the original meeting.

5.2.2 Content of the notice

The notice should name the company and should state the following:

(1) the time, date and place of the meeting;
(2) whether the meeting is an AGM, EGM or other meeting;[2]
(3) any business (see below) which is to be conducted at the meeting, in sufficient detail to enable any member to determine whether he should attend (sometimes an appendix is used, but this may make the notice unwieldy);
(4) the actual text of any special or extraordinary resolutions,[3] or ordinary resolutions in respect of which special notice is required;[4]
(5) details of compensation to be paid to any director for loss of office;[5] and
(6) any resolutions proposed by a members' requisition.[6]

All business should be described in the notice unless the articles say that certain items of business need not be set out in the notice. Older companies often have such a provision in their articles, as older versions of Table A contained a provision which required all 'special business' to be set out in the notice. Special business is usually defined as anything other than the presentation of accounts, the appointment of directors and the appointment of auditors. Unless the articles so provide, there is no requirement that a notice should be read out to, or approved by, the meeting which it calls.

One of the proposals put out for consultation as part of the Company Law Review is whether there should be a statutory agenda for an AGM, which would be likely to include laying the annual accounts and reports, the appointment of auditors (where required), the election and re-election of directors, and the confirmation of appointments made by the board to fill casual vacancies in the board of directors.

---

1   *Wills v Murray* (1850) 4 Exch 843.
2   Companies Act 1985, s 366(1).
3   Companies Act 1985, s 378.
4   See **4.7**.
5   Companies Act 1985, s 312 and see **4.7**.
6   Companies Act 1985, s 376(4); see **5.2.6**.

5.2.3   Authorising the notice

The notice should be signed by a director, secretary or other authorised officer of the company.[1] Typically the notice will be signed by the secretary, but since the proper authority for calling a members meeting is the board,[2] the secretary should include in the notice next to his signature the words 'by order of the board'. These rules are varied in the case of companies which are being wound up or are in insolvency proceedings.

5.2.4   Proxy notices

Although this is not compulsory in the case of a company limited by guarantee, where the articles confer a right to appoint proxies, the notice should also include a statement reminding the member of the right to appoint a proxy. The notice should accurately reflect the provisions of the articles as to the appointment of a proxy and may even refer the member to particular provisions of the articles. It is also good practice to encourage the appointment of proxies by including with the notice of the meeting a blank form of appointment of proxy, which again should reflect any provision in the articles (and see further below). If no form of proxy is specified in the articles, Table A gives a form of proxy which may be used. Companies which have taken advantage of s 30 of the Companies Act 1985 should be careful accurately to state the name of the company, as Table A refers to the name of the company ending with 'PLC/Limited'.

It is likely that, in the future, companies will be able to allow their members to return proxy forms electronically, although this is a separate development from any proposals that the meeting itself should be able to take place electronically.[3]

5.2.5   Accompanying documents

In the case of a meeting (usually an AGM) at which accounts are to be presented,[4] the directors must send out copies of the annual accounts together with copies of the directors' report, and, unless the company can take advantage of the audit exemptions, copies of the auditor's report. These documents must be sent to every member of the company, every debenture holder and to every person entitled to receive notice.[5] Since they must be sent at least 21 days before the meeting,[6] the usual practice is to send them with the notice, although this is not compulsory.

---

1   Companies Act 1985, ss 41 and 744.

2   *Re Haycraft Gold Reduction Co* [1900] 2 Ch 230; except where a meeting is summoned by the members under s 368(4), or if the articles make no provision for the calling of meetings: Companies Act 1985, s 370(3).

3   DTI consultation paper: *Electronic Communications for Companies: An Order Under the Electronic Communications Bill* (URN 00/626) February 2000.

4   See **4.6.4** for a summary of the rules relating to accounts.

5   Companies Act 1985, s 283(1).

6   Unless all the members agree: Companies Act 1985, s 238(4).

5.2.6 Members' resolutions

Whatever is stated in the articles, a company is obliged to give notice of any members' resolution which has been properly requisitioned in accordance with ss 376 and 377 of the Companies Act 1985 to the members of the company entitled to receive notice of the next AGM. These sections also provide for the circulation of statements of not more than 1,000 words concerning any matter to be dealt with at any meeting, whether this is an AGM or EGM. There are criminal penalties[1] associated with failure to comply with these provisions.

In the case of a company limited by guarantee without a share capital, the minimum level of support needed for a members' resolution to be proposed at a meeting is one-twentieth of the total voting rights held at the date of the requisition.[2] The requisitionists must sign one or more copies of the requisition and deposit them at the registered office within a specified time limit. In the case of a proposed resolution, the time-limit is not less than six weeks before the meeting.[3] If an AGM is called after the date of the requisition, but for a date within six weeks after the deposition, it does not matter that the requisition was not received by the company within the time-limit and the company must consider the resolution at that AGM.[4] If the requisition is not a resolution but simply a statement to be circulated, the time-limit is one week before the meeting.[5] In either case, the requisitionists must deposit a sum reasonably sufficient to meet the company's expenses in giving effect to it.[6]

If a members' requisition is validly deposited, the company must either include the resolution in the notice of AGM or send a copy of it to the members entitled to receive notice.[7] If there are members who are not entitled to receive notice of the meeting, they must also be notified of the general effect of a requisitioned resolution.[8] If it is not practicable to send the notice of the requisition with the notice of meeting it should be sent to the members as soon as practicable afterwards.[9]

The only grounds on which a company may avoid distributing a properly requisitioned statement is if it (or any other person aggrieved) applies to the court for exemption on the grounds that the statement is being used to secure needless publicity for defamatory matter (ie matter which has a libellous or slanderous content). If the court finds that this is the case, it may also order the requisitionists to pay the company's costs.

---

1   See **4.8.2**.
2   Companies Act 1985, s 376(2).
3   Companies Act 1985, s 377(1).
4   Companies Act 1985, s 377(2).
5   Companies Act 1985, s 377(1).
6   Companies Act 1985, s 377(1).
7   Companies Act 1985, s 376(3).
8   Companies Act 1985, s 376(4), although it would appear they need not be notified of a statement.
9   Companies Act 1985, s 376(5).

It is proposed as part of the Company Law Review that the requisitionists should not have to pay the costs of the company if the requisition is received in good time before the meeting, but that the company should be able to refuse to circulate a resolution if it duplicates another resolution proposed for the same meeting or if it covers the same ground as a resolution put to a meeting in the last five years and not passed. It is recognised that the removal of the cost imposed on the requisitionists could lead to an increase in the number of requisitions which are trivial or vexatious. These issues may be dealt with if the law in this area is changed. The right to have a statement circulated may also be confined to the AGM if, indeed, the requirement to have an AGM is to be retained.[1]

5.2.7 Addition of items to the agenda by a member

In a company limited by guarantee which is set up as a trade association, pressure group, or where a members' club is incorporated, the members may feel that they should have a greater involvement in the selection of the topics for discussion at a general meeting, particularly in the case of an AGM which they may see as their chance to express dissatisfaction with the management of the company as a whole. Although a member is entitled to raise questions at an AGM in relation to any matter which is on the agenda, it is only the requisition rules which permit members to add items to the agenda. If the company receives requests for matters to be considered at the AGM, it should insist on strict compliance with the requisition rules. If it does not, there is a danger that the presentation of items by the members will become commonplace, and trivial matters will be raised by the members which should not properly be discussed at a meeting and it will become very difficult for the chairman to perform his job of keeping control of the meeting. If it is desired that the members of a company should have a greater participation in the direction of policy of the company, then some other method of achieving this should be chosen.[2]

5.3 SERVICE OF THE NOTICE

5.3.1 Who should receive the notice?

The notice should be sent (see below) to all members whose names are entered in the register of members,[3] except any members whose entitlement to receive notice is expressly removed by the articles (for example, 'associate members'). Note, however, that the fact that a member does not have a right to vote at a meeting does not by itself mean that he is not entitled to receive notice of it.

1　See **5.1.2**.
2　Some of the possibilities are discussed at **2.12.7**.
3　Companies Act 1985, s 370(2).

If the above rule is not complied with, the meeting will not have been properly constituted and proceedings conducted at it will be void and of no effect,[1] unless this is expressly excused by the articles. It is normally only excused in the case of accidental failure to give notice. Deliberate failure to give notice would be an abuse of power by the directors.[2]

If members are admitted to membership and their names are entered into the register of members after the notice of meeting has been sent out, they remain entitled to receive notice of the meeting and to attend it, unless the articles expressly state that there is to be a cut-off point. If the rate of admission is such that this will give the company a great administrative burden, because admissions are dealt with by the directors, they may decide not to admit the members. However, a company should be very wary of adopting this strategy since it would be easy for it to be construed as a deliberate ploy by the directors to reduce participation in the meeting. If, for example, it is permitted by the articles for members to be admitted only at particular board meetings, it is unlikely to be improper for the company to continue in this manner even if it will mean that some potential members are not permitted to attend the meeting. If members are to be admitted by the general meeting itself, then unless and until the members' names are entered into the register of members then they are not entitled to attend the meeting, unless the articles provide that potential members should be admitted. In this situation, the potential members will not, of course, be parties to the statutory contract constituted by the articles, but the company might be prevented ('estopped') from denying them admission if it has disclosed the contents of the articles to them as part of the admission process. Equally, if potential members have the right to attend the meeting, they do not necessarily have the right to make representations as to why they should be admitted unless, again, this is promised as part of the admission process.

The notice should also be given to the directors if required by the articles, and in any event to the auditors of the company.[3] In some circumstances, notice of members' meetings may need to be given to debenture holders if a change to the company's objects clause is required.[4]

5.3.2 The method of service

Notice must be served in the manner set out in the articles, or, if there is no express provision, in the manner provided by Table A.[5] Unless the articles specifically authorise service by a method of communication such as fax or e-mail, these methods should probably not be used as the law presently stands. However, as part of the reforms of the law to facilitate e-commerce,

1   *Smyth v Darley* (1849) 2 HLC 789.
2   See **4.5.4**.
3   Companies Act 1985, s 391.
4   Companies Act 1985, s 5(8).
5   Companies (Tables A to F) Regulations 1985, SI 1985/805 as amended by SI 1985/1052.

notices distributed by e-mail or even posted on a website may be permitted in the future.[1] Articles may provide for a meeting to be convened by means of an advertisement placed in a newspaper, or by means of a notice in a newsletter sent to all members of the company. If the company does not comply with the provisions of the article (or statutory provisions if there are no provisions in the articles) as to the service of notices, the meeting will not be valid, although a member who turns up at the meeting will be taken to have waived his right to complain about the irregularity.[2]

If a meeting is called by the court, the court may give directions as to the calling of the meeting.[3] There are additional requirements in the case of meetings called as part of a members' voluntary winding up.[4]

5.4 HOLDING A MEMBERS' MEETING

5.4.1 The method of holding a meeting

As the law presently stands, there are many obstacles in the way of holding valid meetings by electronic means (such as an internet 'chat' facility). At common law, an electronic 'meeting' probably does not count as a meeting at all. The case of *Byng v London Life Association Ltd and Another*[5] does not constitute authority for the proposition that a meeting may be held entirely by videoconference. In that case the link permitted by video-conference was to an overflow room and at the same time a conventional meeting was taking place with a chairman presiding in the usual way.

Written resolutions[6] may, however, be sent to all the members by e-mail. If the written resolutions are printed out in identical form and signed by every member, they will be valid. Electronic signatures will probably not suffice as the law presently stands, although the matter is not certain. For the sake of a member having to print the resolution, sign it, and put it in the post or deliver it to the company, the risk of an invalid electronic resolution is probably not worth taking. The Electronic Communications Act 2000 provides that in any legal proceedings, electronic signatures are admissible in evidence in relation to a question of the authenticity of the communi-cation or of data contained in it. However, there may still be separate Companies House requirements to be complied with, as the acceptance of documents by the registrar is not 'legal proceedings'.

Methods of holding meetings are specifically addressed in the Company Law Review. The consultation paper *Company General Meetings and*

---

1   See the DTI consultation paper: *Electronic Communications for Companies: An Order Under the Electronic Communications Bill* (URN 00/626) February 2000.
2   *Re British Sugar Refinery Co* [1857] 26 LJ Ch 367.
3   See Companies Act 1985, s 371 and see also s 425(1).
4   Insolvency Act 1986, ss 85 and 89.
5   [1990] Ch 170, [1989] 1 All ER 560, CA.
6   See **5.5.5**.

Shareholder Communication issued in October 1999, considers whether the requirement to hold a meeting should include a requirement that every member should be able to see the other members. It asks whether members' votes may be registered by means of postings on an electronic bulletin board and, if so, whether the bulletin board should be required to be left open for postings for a number of days. It also asks whether an electronic general meeting may be held if the members agree to this in advance and whether approval should be by means of an ordinary or special resolution. In addition, it considers how the quorum requirement should be formulated in the case of a remotely held meeting.

Postal ballots are not meetings and neither do they take effect as written resolutions unless every member agrees to the resolution. The court may, however, order a meeting to be held in any manner authorised by the order. In a case concerning the British Union for the Abolition of Vivisection[1] (a company limited by guarantee), following a meeting of the company that turned into a riot, the committee (board of directors) proposed changes to the articles to allow proxy votes to be cast. However, the meeting to alter the articles also threatened to turn into a riot. The committee petitioned the court to call a meeting under the power contained in s 371 of the Companies Act 1985. The court ordered that only members of the committee should be entitled to attend that meeting, but that the other members of the company should be entitled to cast votes by post.

5.4.2 Quorum

The 'quorum' is the number of members who must be present or represented at a meeting in order for it to be validly constituted. If a quorum is not present, a meeting has no authority to conduct any business. If a meeting which is quorate subsequently becomes inquorate, it ceases to have authority to conduct business, unless there is a provision in the articles (or any rules made pursuant to the articles) which rescues the meeting (for example by providing for an automatic adjournment).[2]

In the absence of any provision in the articles, the quorum at a general meeting of a company (other than a company with a single member) is two members present personally (rather than represented by proxies).[3] At common law, one person cannot constitute a meeting,[4] and this rule will apply whenever there is more than one member entered in the register of members, even if the single person present holds proxies for several members.[5] Unless otherwise stated in the articles setting the quorum, proxy votes do not count towards a quorum. However, if the company has a single member, s 370A of the Companies Act 1985 provides that whatever is

---

1   *Re British Union for the Abolition of Vivisection* [1995] 2 BCLC 1, ChD.
2   Or a petition is made to the court under s 371 of the Companies Act 1985.
3   Companies Act 1985, s 370(4).
4   *Sharp v Dawes* (1876) 2 QBD 26.
5   *Re Sanitary Carbon Co* [1877] WN 223.

stated in the articles, one member present in person or by proxy constitutes a quorum. A quorum of one may also be authorised by the court where a meeting is called by the court under s 371 of the Companies Act 1985 or by the Secretary of State when calling a meeting in default of an AGM under s 367 of the Companies Act 1985.

The articles may allow a non-member holding proxy votes to be counted in the quorum, but at common law a person must be entitled to vote at a meeting in order to be counted towards its quorum.[1] A representative of a corporate member[2] is treated as personally present and is not treated like a proxy.[3]

In a company limited by guarantee, it is often thought to be a good idea to provide for a relatively high quorum in order to ensure that there is a high degree of participation in the conduct of the company's business. However, care should be taken when drafting the articles to ensure that a decline in membership will not lead to the company becoming deadlocked. For example, the quorum could be set at a (fairly low) number of members or a percentage of the total number of members, whichever is the higher.

Where there are different classes of membership, it is also possible to provide for the quorum at general meetings to be composed of a minimum number or percentage of members of a particular class. Again, however, there is the possibility that the membership of a particular class may decline below the level of the quorum and this possibility should be considered when drafting.

If the company does not adopt the conventional 'one member, one vote' scheme for voting at general meetings, this does not have any effect on the quorum. To take an extreme example, a meeting of a company of more than one member, at which only ordinary resolutions were to be proposed, would not be quorate if attended only by a single member having 51 per cent of the votes.

Where the management and activities of a company limited by guarantee are not controversial, it may sometimes be difficult for a company to achieve a quorum at its meetings. This is particularly the case where the quorum is set at a percentage of the total number of members, and the membership expands continually each year but where the new members are not necessarily interested in active participation in the affairs of the company. The members may have joined because this was a necessary precondition to obtaining some particular benefit (for example, the use of facilities at a club). If this is the case, the company should consider introducing some incentive to attend meetings, such as timing meetings so as to precede a social function. Provided that the incentive is within the objects and powers of the company, there is nothing improper in using

---

1   *Young v South African Syndicate* [1896] 2 Ch 268.
2   Companies Act 1985, s 375.
3   *In re Kelantan Cocoa Nut Estates Ltd* [1920] WN 274.

incentives in order toencourage a wider participation in the meeting. However, the directors' power to select the time and place of the meeting should, like all their powers, be exercised in good faith in the interests of the company. The directors should not choose a time which they know to be inconvenient for the members in order to attempt to pass resolutions which might not secure a broad mandate.[1]

5.4.3 The chairman

Every meeting should have a chairman. The appointment of a chairman is usually governed by the articles and, conventionally, the chairman of the board of directors will serve as the chairman of general meetings of the company. The articles should provide for the possibility that the nominated person might be absent from the meeting. It is usually provided that in the absence of the chairman, another member of the board may take the chair. If the articles do not provide for the appointment of a chairman, the company is governed by s 370(5) of the Companies Act 1985 which provides for the members present to elect one of their number to be chairman. The chairman is the representative of the members and not the directors, even where he is also chairman of the board.

The chairman must act fairly at all times, and must give all members the opportunity to speak on any matter within the business of the meeting as defined by the notice. He should also regulate the taking of polls, and put to the vote of the meeting any proposal which should properly be put to it, including a proposal to amend an ordinary resolution.[2] The chairman's overriding duty is to ascertain the wishes of the meeting.[3] The chairman may order anything to be done which is necessary for this purpose unless the matter is specifically dealt with in the Companies Act 1985, the articles or by-laws, or established practices of the company governing proceedings at members' meetings. The chairman must also preserve order, and prevent interruptions to speeches. If a vocal minority is wasting time by making lengthy speeches, or is otherwise attempting to disrupt the meeting, the chairman should propose to the meeting that discussion should be called to an end. It may be sensible to set time-limits for speeches, and to state this in the notice of meeting. The chairman should also bear in mind that speeches made in the course of company meetings are not automatically privileged in the law of defamation, and it would be proper for a chairman to prevent a member from continuing with a defamatory speech.[4]

Although the chairman has the right to refuse admission to a meeting of members of the public, the press, interested observers and the like, he is not entitled to expel a member entitled to attend the meeting unless the

---

1   *Cannon v Trask* (1875) LR 20 Eq 669.
2   There can be no amendments made to special or extraordinary resolutions: see **5.5.2**.
3   *National Dwelling Society v Sykes* [1894] 3 Ch 159.
4   For a discussion of the law of defamation as applied to company meetings, see Impey *Company Meetings* 24th edn (Jordans, 1999).

meeting is threatened by that member's disorderly conduct. The chairman should ascertain that expulsion is supported by the other members present. If it is so supported, reasonable force may be used to expel a disorderly member.

The power to adjourn a meeting rests with the members at common law.[1] Generally, the articles of a company will set out the procedure for adjourning a meeting and will typically give the chairman of the meeting the authority to decide that a meeting should be adjourned. It is proposed as part of the Company Law Review to amend the general rule and to confine the power to adjourn to the chairman, to avoid the abuse of power by disruptive minorities at company meetings.

The chairman's power to adjourn is a fiduciary power and must be exercised in the best interests of the company. A meeting may also be adjourned by the court in exceptional circumstances. At common law, no notice of an adjourned meeting is necessary,[2] but the articles will normally legislate on this point.

There is no general principle that a chairman has a casting vote, but the articles will often provide that the chairman has a casting vote in the event of an equality of votes. Unless the company has so few members that an exact count can be made on a show of hands, generally a chairman should not exercise the casting vote unless he has called a poll and this has shown there to be an equality of votes. The chairman is not obliged to exercise the casting vote but, if he chooses to do so, it must be exercised in the best interests of the company as a whole. The chairman should distinguish between this casting vote and any vote to which he may be entitled as a member.

Generally, the chairman's decisions will bind the company unless they are overturned by the company in general meeting or by the court. In the case of special or extraordinary resolutions, s 378(4) of the Companies Act 1985 provides that a declaration by the chairman that the resolution is carried is conclusive evidence of that fact, unless a poll is demanded, and the chairman is not obliged to record the number of votes for and against the resolution. The chairman's duty to ascertain the wishes of the meeting will, however, usually require that a poll should be called for these types of resolution unless the show of hands suggests the meeting is almost unanimous either way.

5.4.4   Voting on a show of hands

Most votes determined at a company general meeting are decided by a show of hands. On a show of hands, an individual has only one vote even if the articles give weighted voting rights in the case of a poll.

---

1   *National Dwelling Society v Sykes* [1894] 3 Ch 159; and note that at common law a meeting does not have this power unless it is quorate.
2   *Wills v Murray* (1850) 4 Exch 843.

The chairman of a meeting may be faced with the situation where some people present in the room are not entitled to vote on a show of hands. The chairman should adopt some method of determining who is entitled to vote so that he counts all valid votes and does not count any purported votes from non-members. If there are very few non-members, it may be sufficient for these to be identified to the chairman individually, or for them to be required to sit in a clearly defined area which the chairman can readily discount when considering the views of members. Alternatively, coloured 'for' and 'against' voting cards may be given to members to indicate their votes on a show of hands. Whatever method is chosen the chairman should remember that it is his duty to ascertain the wishes of the meeting, which means the people entitled to vote and not those who are non-voting observers.

5.4.5 The right to demand a poll

The articles may set out a code governing the entitlement to demand a poll. This may not be more restrictive than the code contained in s 373 of the Companies Act 1985, although it may be more generous. Section 373 provides that a poll may be demanded by at least five members entitled to vote, or members holding 10 per cent or more of the total voting rights. In a company limited by guarantee and having a share capital, members holding shares on which 10 per cent or more of the total paid-up share capital has been paid may also demand a poll. If the company's articles permit the appointment of proxies, a person who holds proxy votes may also demand a poll.[1] The articles of a company limited by guarantee will often be generous on the question of rights to demand a poll, for example by giving this right to less than the minimum number or proportion of members set out above. Section 373 does not confer upon the chairman the right to demand a poll, although this power is commonly given by the articles. If there is no power in the articles and the chairman considers that a poll is desirable, he should propose to the meeting that a poll should be taken.

Two relaxations of the code contained in s 373 permitted by the Act are the question of the appointment of the chairman and the question of the adjournment of the meeting. The articles may provide that the members have no right to demand a poll on these questions. The usual provision is that a poll on these questions is to be taken immediately and not as the chairman directs.

If a poll is validly demanded, the chairman must allow a poll as, otherwise, the resolution in question is void. The articles may allow the demand for a poll to be withdrawn.

---

1   Companies Act 1985, s 373(2).

5.4.6   Methods of taking a poll

Unless the articles make express provision for the method in which the poll is taken, the poll is to be taken as the chairman directs and should not be taken in such a manner as to be inconvenient to the members. It is sensible for the chairman to direct a time for the poll to be closed. If the poll is postponed this is not a postponement or adjournment of the meeting itself, which may be a relevant question when considering the admissibility of proxies.

A poll is usually taken by means of voting slips which should be signed or otherwise authenticated by the member or proxy. If the company's articles do not follow the 'one member, one vote' principle, the voting slips should reflect this. If there is more than one resolution to be put to the poll, the voting slips should allow each resolution to be voted on separately. It is good practice for a chairman to appoint scrutineers to check the voting slips; the company's auditors will often undertake this task.

On a poll taken at a meeting of a company or at a meeting of any class of members of a company, a member holding more than one vote need not use all the votes or cast all the votes in the same way.[1] The articles will usually provide for a poll on the question of electing a chairman or of adjourning the meeting to be taken immediately and for a poll on any other question to be taken as directed by the chairman. It may be permissible for polling papers to be sent to members by post for return by post but only if there is a specific provision to this effect in the articles. This is because the poll is an extension of the meeting at which it was demanded and a postal ballot is not normally regarded as a meeting. Otherwise, the chairman must set a place, date and time for the holding of the poll and members and their proxies must attend in person.

McMillan v Le Roi Mining Co[2] concerned the construction of a company's articles which provided that a poll should be taken in such manner as the chairman directed. The chairman directed that there should be a poll taken by means of polling papers sent out to the members of the company to be returned by a certain time on a certain date. This was held to be incorrect and an evasion of the proxy machinery, since the papers were sent out to members who had not been at the meeting. The chairman's motive might have been to try to secure a vote in favour of the amalgamation of the company, a proposal which had been clearly rejected on a show of hands at the meeting.

The company may wish to conduct a poll using the single transferable vote,[3] for example where there are more candidates for the office of director than there are vacancies. The single transferable vote requires the voter to give an order of preference for each candidate, so that he is not asked to decide

---

1   Companies Act 1985, s 374.
2   [1906] 1 Ch 331.
3   As promoted by The Electoral Reform Society of Great Britain.

only a yes or no question in relation to each director. There appears to be nothing in the law relating to companies limited by guarantee that prohibits this course of action provided that a poll is validly demanded and the chairman directs that the election should be held by means of the single transferable vote. In the case of a public company, there is a specific prohibition, in s 292 of the Companies Act 1985, on voting on the election of several directors by means of a single resolution. This was designed to avoid the board giving members the choice of electing all the directors or none of them. This provision does not apply to private companies.

5.4.7 Proxies

Unless provided in the articles, proxies are not permitted at meetings of members of a company limited by guarantee or of meetings of classes of its members.[1] It is, therefore, necessary to make express provision for the appointment of proxies and it is advisable to do so unless the company is likely to be composed mainly of individuals and it is to be the policy that personal attendance is necessary.

If the board does decide to send out forms of proxy with the notice of meeting,[2] all members entitled to vote must be sent an identical proxy form. The board may even use the power to send out proxy forms worded in such a way as to influence votes in favour of the board's policy (for example, to vote in favour of a proposed change to the constitution), provided that this course of action can be defended as being in the best interests of the company.[3] The articles may not provide for the proxy forms to be required to be received by the company more than 48 hours before the time set for the meeting.[4]

Since proxies are only permitted if the articles allow, the right to appoint a proxy is a contractual right and any terms in the articles as to its exercise must be strictly observed.[5] The proxy is the agent of the appointing member and the member may revoke the proxy's authority by turning up at the meeting in person.[6] However, if the member changes his mind as to the person to appoint as proxy, the revocation of the first proxy is effective only if the company receives evidence that shows that the member intended to revoke the proxy.[7]

It is usual to provide that proxies may vote only on a poll and not on a show of hands because of the difficulty of counting proxy votes on a show of hands. In the case of a company limited by shares, this is also the position if

---

1   Companies Act 1985, s 372(2)(a).

2   See **5.2.4**.

3   *Peel v London and North Western Railway Co* [1907] 1 Ch 5.

4   Companies Act 1985, s 372(5).

5   *Harben v Phillips* (1883) 23 ChD 14.

6   *Cousins v International Brick Co Ltd* [1931] 2 Ch 90.

7   See Impey *Company Meetings* 24th Edn (Jordans, 1999) at pp 76–81.

the articles are silent on the point,[1] and probably the position is the same in a company limited by guarantee.[2] This also means that non-members may not vote on a show of hands. It is always open to the chairman of a meeting to order a poll to be taken where he thinks this is necessary in order to give effect to the wishes of the meeting. Where there are a large number of proxy votes, it would normally be appropriate to call a poll. Even if the articles allow proxies a vote on a show of hands, the proxy will have only one vote however many votes he represents on a poll.[3] It is proposed as part of the Company Law Review that this rule should be changed, although the particular case of a company limited by guarantee is not discussed in the consultation paper. The reasoning behind the proposal for reform is that proxy votes are often ignored by companies by deciding matters on a show of hands.

5.4.8 Representatives of corporations

Since a corporation must act by human representatives, the Companies Act 1985 provides for attendance at meetings by representatives. This is separate from any right to appoint proxies conferred on the corporation by the articles. A corporation (which for this purpose includes statutory corporations and bodies incorporated by Royal Charter) may by a resolution of its directors or other governing body appoint any person to act as its representative at meetings of the company or at any class meetings or (if it is a creditor) at meetings of the company's creditors.[4] In the case of a company limited by guarantee, it is possible to exclude or limit the right to appoint proxies and the articles may permit only individual members to appoint proxies.

5.4.9 Visitors

In a company limited by guarantee, it may be the case that non-members wish to attend a general meeting of the company as observers. Apart from directors of the company, who are entitled to attend the meetings even if they are not also members, non-members have no right to attend meetings of the company. It is for the meeting to decide whether or not non-members should be admitted, and the chairman should take a vote to ascertain the wishes of the meeting.[5]

---

1   Companies Act 1985, s 372(2)(c).
2   Section 372(2)(a) of the Companies Act 1985 provides that the default power to appoint proxies does not apply if the company does not have a share capital, but the same restriction does not appear in s 372(2)(c).
3   *Ernest v Loma Gold Mines* [1897] 1 Ch 1.
4   Companies Act 1985, s 375.
5   *Carruth v Imperial Chemical Industries Ltd* [1937] AC 707, [1937] 2 All ER 422, HL.

5.5 TYPES OF MEMBERS' RESOLUTIONS

5.5.1 Ordinary resolutions

Most company resolutions are ordinary resolutions, which are passed if a simple majority of the members present and voting at the meeting vote in favour. There are some instances in the Companies Act 1985 where an ordinary resolution is required. In the case of a company limited by guarantee the most important is the right to remove a director under s 303 of the Companies Act 1985. It should be noted that special notice is required of a resolution to remove a director or auditor.[1] Generally, anything which requires a decision by the company and which the company has not delegated to the directors may be decided by an ordinary resolution unless another type of resolution is required by statute.

Ordinary resolutions do not need to be set out in detail in the notice of meeting and amendments may be made at a meeting itself after a particular form of resolution has been proposed to the meeting. Any amendments may be proposed by the chairman or by a member and are not required to be seconded.[2]

However, the members must understand the effect of the proposed change and the change must not take the resolution outside the scope of the business disclosed in the notice. This is because the notice is required to give a sufficient indication of the business to be conducted at the meeting to enable a member to decide whether to attend. An amendment which goes beyond what is described in the notice might have affected that decision and denied a member the opportunity to vote.

5.5.2 Special resolutions

Special resolutions are required by the Companies Act 1985 for specific decisions of a fundamental constitutional nature, ie for changes to the objects,[3] name,[4] articles[5] and provisions of the memorandum which could have been in the articles.[6] Special resolutions are also required by certain provisions of the Insolvency Act 1986. The articles may require certain decisions to be made by a special resolution, although the articles cannot require a special resolution for the removal of a director.[7]

The minimum notice period is 21 days, even if the special resolution is to be proposed at an extraordinary general meeting which would otherwise only require 14 days. The articles may provide for a longer notice period. The entire text of the resolution should be set out in the notice of meeting and no

---

1   See **4.7**.
2   *Re Horbury Bridge Coal Co* (1879) 11 ChD 109.
3   Companies Act 1985, s 4.
4   Companies Act 1985, s 28.
5   Companies Act 1985, s 9.
6   Companies Act 1985, s 17.
7   Companies Act 1985, s 303 and see **4.7**.

amendments may be made at the meeting unless these are necessary to correct obvious grammatical or typographical errors, or if all the members of the company entitled to vote agree to the change.[1] The notice should also identify the resolution as being proposed as a special resolution.

A special resolution is passed if three-quarters of the members voting on a show of hands are in favour of the resolution, or if a poll is held, if three-quarters of the votes cast are in favour of the resolution. An abstention is not a vote cast and so abstentions are not counted in the relevant calculation. (It is possible that in future legislation there will be a requirement for a company to recognise abstentions when declaring the results of a vote, or perhaps this may be recommended as good practice.) Proxies will be included if they are permitted by the articles but will only count on a show of hands if the articles specifically authorise this.

5.5.3 Extraordinary resolutions

Extraordinary resolutions are required for insolvent winding up[2] and in the case of a members' voluntary winding up, for sanctioning the exercise of the liquidator's powers.[3] If the company limited by guarantee has share capital divided into classes of shares, the variation of the class rights will also require an extraordinary resolution.[4] In future, it is possible that the provisions of the Companies Act 1985 which require an extraordinary resolution may be amended so that a special resolution is required.

If the resolution is proposed at an EGM (as will usually be the case) 14 days' notice is required. If the meeting is an AGM, 21 days' notice will be required in any event. The articles may require a longer period of notice. The rules as to the content of the notice and amendments to the resolution are the same as for special resolutions, as are the rules relating to the majority required to pass an extraordinary resolution.

5.5.4 Elective resolutions

Elective resolutions are resolutions required for specific purposes allowed by the Companies Act 1985. Since they relax certain statutory provisions, they must be passed by all the members of the company.[5] Note that, even if a meeting is held, all the members entitled to attend and vote must be present in person or by proxy (if the articles permit proxies) and must all vote in favour of the resolution and not abstain. In the case of a new company limited by guarantee which is intended to have a large membership, therefore, it would be appropriate to consider whether the elective resolutions should be passed by the subscriber members before the admission of a large number of additional members.

---

1   *Re Moorgate Mercantile Holdings Ltd* [1980] 1 WLR 227, ChD.
2   Insolvency Act 1986, s 84(1)(c).
3   Insolvency Act 1986, s 165(2)(a).
4   Companies Act 1985, s 125(2).
5   Companies Act 1985, s 379A(2).

Elective resolutions relevant to a company limited by guarantee and not having a share capital are as follows:

(1) to dispense with the laying of accounts and reports before a general meeting;[1]
(2) to dispense with annual general meetings[2] (note that these first two are separate resolutions, as accounts may be laid other than at an AGM);
(3) to reduce the majority required to authorise short notice of a meeting;[3]
(4) to dispense with the annual appointment of auditors.[4]

At least 21 days' notice is required for an elective resolution[5] and, as with special and extraordinary resolutions, the text of the resolution must be set out in the notice and cannot normally be amended unless all the members agree.[6] In any event, the text is in fairly standard form. Since all the members must agree, in the case of a company with a small membership it may be more convenient for the resolutions to be passed as written resolutions. Any elective resolution may be revoked by an ordinary resolution.[7]

5.5.5 Written resolutions

If all the members who are entitled to vote agree on a particular resolution, it will be valid and binding upon the company.[8] This matches general contract law in that a contract may be varied by the agreement of all the parties. However, this doctrine of informal corporate acts may only be used to authorise something which is not beyond the powers of the company as set out in the memorandum and cannot be used to authorise changes to the memorandum that are not permitted by the Companies Act 1985.[9] Neither is it safe to rely on the informal agreement principle where the decision is one which could affect the interests of the company's creditors.[10]

The common law principle is now put on a statutory basis by s 381A of the Companies Act 1985: anything which may be passed by the general meeting (whether as an ordinary, special, extraordinary, or elective resolution) or by any class of members of the company may be done without a meeting and without notice, by means of a resolution in writing signed by or on behalf of all the members of the company who at the date of the resolution would be entitled to attend and vote at such meeting. The signatures may be on

---

1   Companies Act 1985, s 252.
2   Companies Act 1985, s 366A.
3   Companies Act 1985, s 369(4) and s 378(3).
4   Companies Act 1985, s 386.
5   Unless the requisite majority agrees to the calling of the meeting on short notice: see **5.2.1**.
6   Companies Act 1985, s 379A(2).
7   Companies Act 1985, s 379A(3)
8   *Re Duomatic Ltd* [1969] 2 WLR 114, *Wright v Atlas Wright (Europe) Ltd* (1999) *The Times*, February 3.
9   Companies Act 1985, s 2(7).
10   *Re R W Peak (Kings Lynn) Ltd* [1998] 1 BCLC 193.

separate pieces of paper provided that the text of the resolution is accurately stated on each copy.

A written resolution passed under s 381A may not be used to remove a director or an auditor. This is because of the requirement to give special notice and for the director or auditor to have the opportunity to make representations.[1] Schedule 15A to the Companies Act 1985 also modifies procedural requirements where a written resolution is used for certain purposes.[2] Written resolutions must be recorded in the minute book as if they were minutes of a meeting,[3] and in particular the original signatures should be inserted in the minute book.

The written resolution must be copied to the auditor at or before the time when the resolution is supplied to a member for signature,[4] but the former requirement that the auditor had to give *prior* approval to the resolution has been abolished. The requirement does not apply to a company which is exempt from the obligation to appoint auditors.

The articles may provide for a written resolution to be valid and may prescribe a different procedure. In particular, under the articles, there may be no requirement to consult the auditors. The Companies Act 1985 does not invalidate such an article but it is better to use the statutory code, since there may be some doubt as to whether the provision in the articles will permit the passing of an elective resolution, or any other resolution required to be considered 'by the company in general meeting'. Section 381A specifically authorises the use of the statutory written resolution procedure in these cases.

5.6 POST-MEETING STEPS

The company secretary should comply with the provisions of s 380 of the Companies Act 1985 which require copies of certain resolutions to be filed at Companies House. Copies of any resolutions amending the articles should be annexed to the articles, or the changes should be incorporated into a new version of the articles.[5] Changes to the memorandum or articles must always be notified to the Registrar of Companies[6] and companies should file both a copy of the resolution (which should be authenticated on behalf of the company, usually by the secretary) and a copy of the articles as amended. Section 380 also applies to any other special resolution, and all extraordinary and elective resolutions, together with written resolutions

---

1   See **4.7**.
2   For example, the approval of a director's service contract under s 319: see **4.6.1**.
3   Companies Act 1985, s 382A.
4   Companies Act 1985, s 381B.
5   Companies Act 1985, s 380(2).
6   See Companies Act 1985, ss 6 and 18.

passed where a special, extraordinary, or elective resolution is required by the Companies Act 1985 or the articles.

There may also be forms required by specific sections of the Act to be completed and filed at Companies House as a result of the decision at the meeting. The secretary should also ensure that any necessary entries are made in the statutory books, such as adding to the register of members details of any new members admitted at the meeting, or updating the register of directors.

The secretary should also write up the minutes after the meeting, as required by s 382 of the Companies Act 1985. Minutes should be an accurate record of proceedings at the meeting but it is not necessary to record full details of every speech or argument. Full details of every resolution passed should, however, be included. The minutes should be signed by the chairman of the meeting minuted, or the next following meeting. If signed in this way, the minutes constitute evidence of the proceedings at the meeting, and the meeting is deemed to have been duly held.[1] The secretary must not make any alterations to the minutes once signed, even if he realises that they are incorrect. The correct procedure is for the amendment to be considered at the next meeting and for any alterations to be made and signed by the chairman. If there is any dispute, the alterations must only be such as to ensure accuracy of the minutes.

Minutes should be kept in a minute book, commonly part of a bound volume or ring binder of 'statutory books' bought from a legal stationer. The pages should be numbered, particularly where the books are loose-leaf or where wordprocessed minutes are printed out and inserted into the book. The minutes may be kept on disk as long as they are capable of being reproduced in legible form,[2] but it is not thought to be good practice to keep minutes in electronic form only. The minute book must be kept at the registered office (there is an exception for minutes of meetings held before 1 November 1929). It must be open to inspection by any member without charge, for not less than two hours between the hours of 9am and 5pm on each business day (ie weekdays, excluding bank and public holidays), and a member must be permitted to take notes or transcribe the minutes. A member may also demand copies of entries in the minutes on payment of the prescribed fee (currently 10 pence per 100 words or part of 100).The company must supply the copies within seven days after the request. The company and any officer in default is liable to a fine if the inspection rules are not complied with. A non-member may not inspect the minutes. Members have no right to inspect the minutes of directors' meetings, so it is preferable to keep separate sets of minutes for general meetings and board meetings.

---

1   Companies Act 1985, s 382(2) and (4).
2   Companies Act 1985, s 723.

5.7 DIRECTORS' MEETINGS

5.7.1 General requirements

Every meeting should have a chairman and the articles will normally provide for the directors to appoint one of their number to be the chairman and for that person to chair both meetings of the board and general meetings of the company. Subject to what is said in the articles, the chairman may be appointed for a particular meeting only or for all meetings and the minutes of the first meeting should record which is the case. If there is no provision in the articles for the appointment of chairman, those present at a quorate meeting may elect a chairman themselves.

The board must make decisions collectively, which means that it must either meet or make decisions by means of a unanimous written resolution. A written resolution is permitted even if the articles do not contain an express provision permitting such resolutions. If, in an emergency, a decision needs to be taken quickly, it can be ratified at a subsequent quorate board meeting.

A company must have at least one director, and a company secretary must not also be the sole director. In other words, there will always be at least two different people appointed as officers of the company. It is now thought that the presence of a sole director can constitute a meeting, even though at common law at least two people are required to form a meeting.[1] However, in practice it would be sensible for a sole director to call the secretary to a board meeting so that the secretary can take minutes, as the minutes of the meeting are an important record showing that the director has complied with certain requirements of the Companies Act 1985.[2]

5.7.2 Calling a directors' meeting

The method of calling a directors' meeting is determined by the usual practice of the company. Written notice is not required unless this is established as the usual practice or if it is required by the articles.[3] Likewise, the period of notice required is determined by custom and practice, and it is perfectly proper for an emergency meeting to be summoned at a moment's notice if all the directors can be contacted and are able to attend. Deliberate exclusion of a director (for example, at a meeting at which it was proposed to call a general meeting of the company to force the director out of office) would not be a proper use of the board's power to call meetings. Generally, notice should be given to all directors even if the secretary has already received information from a particular director that he is unable to attend a meeting. The only possible exception to the notice requirement is if a

---

1   *Neptune (Vehicle Washing Equipment) Ltd v Fitzgerald* [1995] 3 WLR 108, ChD.
2   The *Neptune* case itself concerned the requirement of s 317 of the Companies Act 1985 to disclose interests in contracts made by the company, breach of which attracts a criminal sanction.
3   *Browne v La Trinidad* (1887) 37 ChD 1.

practice is established by which meetings are always held at the same time and in the same place and at regular intervals. However, it is useful for every meeting to have an agenda and ideally this should be circulated in advance.

The rules for the calling of directors' meetings are much less strict than those for the calling of members' meetings and it is thought that is permissible for the company to call meetings of the board by means such as e-mail. In many cases, this may clearly be in the best interests of the company as it may be the most effective means of communicating with the board members. However, if there is an existing practice of calling meetings by means of a paper notice, all the directors should agree before any change is made to this practice. There may also be occasions when security concerns require a more conventional method of communicating with the directors.

5.7.3 Electronic meetings

Generally the directors of a company may choose how they hold their meetings and meetings may generally be held in informal circumstances provided the correct notice is given. If the board is small enough, a telephone conference where each member of the board can hear each of the others may be an adequate meeting, although this should be authorised by a provision in the articles. However, it is uncertain whether, in the absence of unanimous approval, electronic facilities such as bulletin boards can constitute a meeting. Probably it is best to assume that under the present law they do not.

5.7.4 Quorum at directors' meetings

The articles may provide for a quorum of one.[1] If the articles do not fix the quorum then it is half the number of appointed directors[2]. The quorum is required to be maintained throughout the meeting unless the articles expressly address this point. This can be very significant where a director is required not to vote on a matter in which he is interested,[3] since only members who are entitled to vote are counted for the purposes of the quorum.

5.7.5 Voting

Unless the articles provide otherwise, each director present at a meeting or represented by an alternate has one vote, and decisions are made by means of a simple majority vote. A director may not vote on a matter in which he is interested unless permitted to do so by the articles, although this does not mean that he cannot attend the meeting.[4] The articles cannot, however,

---

1   *Re Fireproof Doors* [1916] 2 Ch 142
2   Contrast the position with members' meetings where the quorum in the absence of express provision is always two: Companies Act 1985, s 370.
3   See **4.5.6**.
4   *Grimwade v BPD Syndicate* (1915) 31 TLR 531.

remove the requirement on the director to declare the nature of his interest at the meeting[1] and this declaration should be recorded in the minutes.

5.7.6   Minutes

Minutes should be taken of all meetings of the board of directors and of all meetings of committees of the board. They should be a complete and accurate record of the business transacted at the meeting. It is usual to state which directors are present at the meeting and note if any others are present (the secretary, for example, or non-voting observers: two separate lists should be given to distinguish the two types of attendees). In all but the most routine of matters, it is good practice to note the number of votes for and against a particular resolution and a director may ask that his opposition to a particular motion should be noted in the minutes.

Minutes of directors' meetings should be authenticated and altered in the same manner as for minutes of members' meetings.[2] The members of a company have no automatic right to inspect the minutes of directors' meetings, or minutes of committee meetings, but every director has the right to inspect the minutes while he holds the office of director. It is not a requirement of the Companies Act 1985 that the minutes of a previous meeting must be circulated to the board for approval. However, approval of the minutes of a previous invalid meeting at a properly convened board meeting may correct the defects in the original meeting.[3]

---

1   Companies Act 1985, s 317.
2   See **5.6**.
3   *Municipal Mutual Insurance Ltd v Harrop* [1998] 2 BCLC 540, ChD.

Chapter 6

CAPITAL, DISTRIBUTIONS AND WINDING UP

6.1 INTRODUCTION

If a company limited by guarantee undergoes some form of insolvency procedure, the control of the company is taken out of the hands of the directors and is given to an insolvency practitioner, who will call in the company's assets, satisfy the claims of the relevant creditors and (in the case of a winding up) distribute any surplus to the members of the company or as directed by the memorandum. Insolvency proceedings are not discussed further in this book. However, where the company is solvent the members of the company may wish to extract value from the company, to reorganise it in some way, or to amalgamate it with another company. The function of this chapter is to look at the issues which are involved and in outline to describe the procedures that may be necessary. It is anticipated that specialist tax advice will need to be taken in each case; this should be done at an early stage as in many cases prior clearance of a scheme by the Inland Revenue may be necessary in order to come within a relevant exemption.

Finally, this chapter considers the winding up of a solvent company, and the removal of a dormant company from the register of companies.

It should be noted in the case of procedures designed to extract cash or other assets from the company that it may, in many cases, be possible to remove the not-for-profit clauses in the memorandum if (as is usually the case) they have not been entrenched.[1] This would then allow a distribution of the assets to the members. However, even if this is legally possible, it may not be possible in practice: the support of at least three-quarters of the voting members is required in order to effect such a change and, in addition, an aggrieved member can petition the court to revoke the change.[2] Removal of the not-for-profit clauses would not, of course, be permitted in the case of a company registered as a charity or as a social landlord.

6.2 THE NATURE OF CAPITAL IN A COMPANY LIMITED BY GUARANTEE

Although many companies limited by guarantee have no need for working capital, the question may arise as to whether a particular contribution made

---

1 See **2.8.7**.
2 Companies Act 1985, s 17(1).

by a member of the company is a contribution to the capital of the company or a loan to the company. In the case of a loan, the member owns the money, but in the case of capital the company owns the money, subject only to the right of the member to receive a proportion of any assets of the company which are not used up in paying off the company's creditors on a winding up.

A case before the Special Commissioner of the Inland Revenue[1] addressed this issue in interpreting a particular provision of the corporation tax legislation. A company limited by guarantee and not having a share capital was set up to provide insurance on a mutual basis. It had two classes of members: ordinary members and founder members. Ordinary members who deposited at least £1,000 with the company became founder members, and the company could not start trading unless the company had deposits of at least £40,000. A provision of the Income and Corporation Taxes Act 1988 concerning loss relief within groups of companies referred to a section containing a definition of ordinary share capital as 'issued share capital, by whatever name called'. It was necessary, in order for the claim to succeed, for the deposits made by the founder members to be 'ordinary share capital' as defined. The Special Commissioner considered whether the deposits were capital, whether they were share capital, and whether they were issued share capital.

On the basis of a nineteenth century case,[2] the Special Commissioner decided that the capital of a company is the money subscribed pursuant to the memorandum or what is represented by that money. One of the reasons for rejecting the argument that the contributions of the founder members were capital was that these contributions were not subscribed pursuant to the memorandum but were required by the articles dealing with the admission and classes of members. In addition, some of the articles of the company treated the payments as debts and not as capital. Even if the deposits were capital, they could not be share capital because there was no division of the capital into shares or interests, and they could not therefore be issued share capital.

6.3 MAINTENANCE OF CAPITAL AND DIVIDENDS

It is a condition of limited liability that the capital of the company should be applied for the purposes for which the company was formed, and should be available to the company's creditors. To that extent, the capital of the company is exposed to a risk of loss, and therefore the return of capital to the members as a dividend is not possible.

---

1   *South Shore Mutual Insurance Co Ltd v Blair (Inspector of Taxes)* [1999] STC (SCD) 296.
2   *Verner v General & Commercial Investment Trust* [1894] 2 Ch 239, CA.

Every distribution of assets to the members of a company limited by guarantee, whether in cash or in kind, other than on a winding up, must comply with the provisions of Part VIII of the Companies Act 1985. A company may only make a distribution to its members out of profits available for the purpose.[1] This means, broadly, accumulated realised profits less accumulated realised losses,[2] which are to be determined by reference to a set of accounts of the company containing the items set out in s 270 of the Companies Act 1985. Usually, the relevant accounts are the last annual accounts of the company. If the distribution is in the first accounting period of the company, management accounts may be used if they enable a reasonable judgement to be made as to the amounts of the items set out in s 270.

The question of what part of the profits can be treated as realised is an accounting issue and the company's directors should always seek the advice of the company's auditors or accountants before making a distribution. The procedural requirements of the Companies Act 1985 (for example, those relating to auditors' statements) must be strictly observed, in addition to the payment being justified by reference to the accounts.

If a distribution is unlawful, it must be repaid by the members who have received it and who knew or had reasonable grounds for believing that the payment was contrary to the Companies Act 1985.[3] It may also give rise to a claim against the company's directors for breach of their fiduciary duties and an accompanying claim for repayment.

The rules relating to distributions are, of course, only relevant to a company limited by guarantee that does not have a not-for-profit clause in its memorandum or articles. They apply whenever a company wishes to distribute to its members surplus income, or distribute cash following a sale of assets, or distribute assets in kind when the purposes of the company come to an end. A charity is permitted to spend all its income and capital in furtherance of its charitable purposes.

6.4   TAKEOVERS

When a company limited by shares is to be taken over by another company, the new parent company will buy the shares from the shareholders, leaving the assets of the company intact. In a company limited by guarantee without a share capital, this is not possible since the capital value of the company is not represented by a certain number of shares which would form a ready means of ascertaining what value should be given to each shareholder in return for the sale of his shares.

---

1   Companies Act 1985, s 263.
2   There are special provisions in the case of insurance companies.
3   Companies Act 1985, s 277.

It would be possible to conceive of a scheme under which each member of a company limited by guarantee would resign as a member and in return for resignation, would be given a sum of money. The new parent company would be admitted as a member of the company in accordance with the articles of association and the takeover would be complete. This scheme would require either the consent of every member of the company or a scheme of arrangement under s 425 of the Companies Act 1985.

However, it would not always be possible to determine what should be the appropriate sum of money to be paid to each member. In the case of a company limited by guarantee which has a single class of members each having one vote at a general meeting of the company, the company as a whole will be valued and divided by the number of members in order to calculate the amount to be paid to each member as compensation. If on the other hand there are weighted voting rights, it will not be immediately obvious what are the relative values of each type of vote. Should the proportionate share of each member be simply a function of the number of members or should the weight of each vote be reflected in the calculation of compensation? A member of a company limited by guarantee who resigns from the company is giving up more than his vote, although in many cases this incident of his membership will be the most important to him. He is also giving up rights recognised by company law such as the right to have the company's affairs conducted in accordance with the memorandum and articles. Is the nature of these rights necessarily linked to the 'share' of the member in the company's capital value? In the case of the company limited by shares, the cases concerning the rights of the members have shown how the rights of the minority deserve the protection of company law, which suggests that there must be something of value in the membership right which is independent of the share of capital to which that member is entitled.

The fact that a company limited by guarantee may have clauses prohibiting the distribution of profits to members does not, of course, prevent the payment of compensation by a purchaser for the resignations of the members. The not-for-profit clauses only prevent the payment of the company's funds to members and not the payment of a purchaser's funds to the members. However, these clauses can be relevant to the question of what value is to be attributed to the member's 'share' in the company. In the *NFU* case,[1] for example, the court had to apply a provision which required approval by three-quarters 'in value' of the members present and voting at a meeting. The court held that the fact that each member had an entitlement, providing that he remained a member, to a share in the surplus on a winding up, meant that even though the voting rights were unequal, three-quarters in value meant a straight three-quarters of the number of members. On the

1   *Re National Farmers' Union Development Trust Ltd* [1972] 1 WLR 1548, [1973] 1 All ER 135.

other hand, in *Re RAC Motoring Services Ltd*,[1] Neuberger J had to consider what rights were held by members who had such an entitlement on a winding up, in the context of a petition for a scheme of arrangement under s 425 of the Companies Act 1985. In that context, the judge decided that the provisions of the memorandum conferred:

> 'no more than a hope or "spes" that the profits of the Company on a winding up may be vested in the [members of a particular class] whoever they may be at the time. Such a right or spes is dependent upon the members not exercising their entitlement in the meantime to alter ... the memorandum or articles'.

6.5   TRANSFERS OF ASSETS

As an alternative to compensating the members of the company for their resignations, the buyer may instead buy the assets of the company and leave it holding cash assets only. This cash may then be distributed to members if there is no prohibition on this in the memorandum, and provided that it constitutes distributable profits. First, however, the memorandum should be checked to ensure that the company has power to dispose of all its undertaking and if not, the memorandum should be amended to include such a power.[2]

The assets will need to be identified and the method of transferring each of the assets to the buyer should be considered. This is a matter of general property law and each type of asset will need to be considered separately. For example, in the case of land and buildings, a deed of transfer of the legal title will be required to be executed by the company and, in certain circumstances, also by the purchaser. Stock, equipment, and other movable assets can be transferred by delivery (either physically moving the items or handing over the keys with the clear intention to pass title). Book debts, intellectual property and other intangible assets can be transferred by a document in writing (but note that in the case of some types of intellectual property a further document may be needed to complete the transfer at the Patent Office or other relevant national registry). Readers should refer to specialist textbooks on the capital gains tax, income tax, stamp duty and value added tax implications of transfers of assets and the way in which tax liabilities may be mitigated.

Even if the company has the power in its memorandum to dispose of the whole of its undertaking, the directors have only the powers entrusted to them by the articles. In the common form of articles, the directors will be given wide powers to manage the affairs of the company. Those powers must be exercised in the interests of the company as a whole. This means that the sale of assets must be at the full market value and the directors are

---

1   [2000] 1 BCLC 307.
2   See Chapter 2.

under a duty to obtain the best price possible. However, unless the members of the company have already been asked, in effect, to approve the transfer by amending the memorandum to allow a sale of all the assets, it may also be appropriate for the directors to propose the sale to the members of the company in a general meeting and secure a clear mandate for their actions. This should be at an early stage in order that there should be no effort wasted on abortive negotiations. It may be advisable to approach the members a second time once the assets of the company have been valued.

In the case of a charity, it may be possible to avoid the expense of winding up by applying all the assets of the company for charitable purposes and then applying to have the company struck off the register (see below). A power to apply all the assets is implied in the case of a charity but it should be noted that the power extends only to applications of assets within the objects clause of the charity, and not to a similar organisation or to any other charity.

6.6   MEMBERS' VOLUNTARY LIQUIDATION

In a members' voluntary liquidation, the assets of the company are distributed in accordance with the memorandum of association of the company, so it is not necessary for all the assets to be dealt with before starting the procedure. In the case of a company which is a registered social landlord, the consent of the Housing Corporation will be a pre-requisite for this procedure.[1]

A qualified insolvency practitioner should be instructed before the members' voluntary liquidation is started and he will advise on the detailed steps required. A majority of the company's directors must resolve at a board meeting that they will make a statutory declaration of solvency in the prescribed form. This is a document sworn and signed in front of a solicitor (who may be present at the board meeting). The statutory declaration must be sworn not less than five weeks before the date of the meeting at which the resolution to wind up is proposed. The declaration states that the directors have made a full inquiry into the company's affairs and that, having done so, they believe that the company will be able to pay its debts in full within a period not exceeding 12 months from the start of the winding up. The declaration will include a statement of the company's assets and liabilities as at the latest practicable date before making the declaration. The board meeting will also call an extraordinary general meeting (EGM) of the company to propose the special resolution that the company should be wound up. Twenty-one days' notice of the meeting must be given, and the notice of the meeting must set out in full the text of the resolution.[2]

---

1   Housing Act 1996, s 7 and Sch 1, para 13.
2   See **5.5.2**.

After the general meeting, the company secretary must file the following documents at Companies House (and with the Accountant in Bankruptcy in the case of Scottish companies) within 15 days:

- the statutory declaration of solvency;
- forms notifying the resolution to wind up; and
- a copy of the special resolution.

Notice of the special resolution for voluntary winding up of the company must be published in the London Gazette (or the Edinburgh Gazette in the case of Scottish companies) within 14 days after the general meeting. The liquidator will arrange certain advertisements to creditors and may require that the registered office of the company is moved to his office so that post is dealt with promptly.

The above procedure for members' voluntary winding up cannot be used if the company is insolvent, as the directors must truthfully be able to say that the company can pay all its debts within 12 months. If the directors are not able to make this declaration, the winding up becomes a creditors' voluntary winding up. A members' voluntary winding up may become a creditors' voluntary winding up if the liquidator disagrees with the declaration of solvency.

At the end of the liquidation, the liquidator will present an account to final meetings of creditors and members of the company, advertised in the London or Edinburgh Gazette at least one month before the date of the meeting. Within one week after the meeting, the liquidator must send the account to the registrar of companies,[1] together with a return of the final meeting. Unless the court makes an order deferring the dissolution of the company, it is dissolved three months after the return and account are registered at Companies House.

In the case of a company which is a registered social landlord, on any winding up under the Insolvency Act 1986, the remaining assets of the company are transferred to the Housing Corporation, or to another registered social landlord at the Corporation's discretion.[2] If the company is a registered charity, the trustees are under a duty to notify the Charity Commissioners of the completion of the winding up so that the charity can be removed from the register.

6.7 SCHEMES UNDER THE INSOLVENCY ACT 1986, s 110

Where a company is wound up by the members, it may be desirable to transfer assets of the company to another company rather than to distribute

---

1   And the Accountant in Bankruptcy in the case of Scottish companies.
2   Housing Act 1996, s 7 and Sch 1, para 15.

them in kind to the members or to pay out cash. It may be used as a means of 'converting' a company limited by guarantee to a company limited by shares; re-registration is not possible, but shares in the new company can be issued to the members of the old company limited by guarantee. An Insolvency Act 1986, s 110 scheme may also be used to partition a company so that part of its undertaking carries on in a new legal entity.

The scheme must be sanctioned by a separate special resolution of the members of the company.[1] However, unlike schemes under the Companies Act 1985, ss 425 to 427, a s 110 scheme cannot be made binding on dissenting minorities. A member who does not vote in favour of the scheme may, within seven days after the passing of the s 110 resolution, require the liquidator to choose between purchasing the member's interest in the company, or not putting the scheme into effect.[2] Neither does the scheme have the effect of transferring the assets to the new company, which must be done as outlined at **6.5** above. However, unlike schemes under ss 425 to 427, the consent of the court is not required.

6.8 SCHEMES UNDER THE COMPANIES ACT 1985, ss 425 to 427

6.8.1 What may a scheme be used to achieve?

Sections 425 to 427 of the Companies Act 1985 apply to companies limited by guarantee as well as to companies limited by shares, and allow a company to make any compromise or arrangement with its creditors or members or with any class of members, provided that the statutory procedure is followed and the court's consent is obtained. A scheme under ss 425 to 427 allows a company to vary the rights of its members or classes of members, even if the memorandum or articles of the company state that these cannot be altered. The application of these provisions to meetings of creditors is not discussed further in this book, but the principles are broadly the same.

A scheme allows almost any kind of internal reorganisation or restructuring of a company. Provided the correct procedure is followed, the scheme will bind all the members of the company (or class as the case may be), even those who have dissented. A scheme may also allow the transfer of the whole of the undertaking of a company to another entity.

There are, however, some restrictions on the applicability of the provisions. The court will not approve a scheme which is outside the objects of the company; though as seen in Chapter 2, these are now freely alterable by special resolution. *Re Oceanic Steam Navigation Co Ltd*[3] concerned a

---

1   A s 110 scheme may be used as part of a creditors' voluntary winding up, but since this applies when the company is insolvent, it is not considered further here.

2   Insolvency Act 1986, s 111(2).

3   [1939] Ch 41, [1938] 3 All ER 740.

compromise with the creditors of the company, who of course do not have the power to effect an alteration of the memorandum. The court rejected the argument that it had the power, under the provision which is now s 425 of the Companies Act 1985, to authorise, in that case, the disposal of the entire undertaking of the company, which would on the facts of the case have been ultra vires. A power to dispose of the entire undertaking of the company will not be implied by the court.

This may require some 'give and take' on the part of each participant.[1] The court may take into account not only the interests of the members but also other affected persons.[2]

6.8.2 The procedure

The procedure is begun by a petition to the court made by the company or a member. The member need not also be a member of the class which it is desired to bind under the scheme, but he must be shown as a current member in the register of members at the date of application.[3] The court will then order a meeting of the members of the company or members of the class and will direct how the meeting is to be called. A 'class' for the purposes of ss 425 to 427 is not necessarily defined by reference to a class of members as described in the company's memorandum or articles. A class means a group of members whose rights are sufficiently similar that it is possible for them to consult each other with a view to their common interests. The relevant classes are determined by the proposed scheme, so the directors should consider whether the scheme creates different classes of members by treating some members differently from others, or whether differing rights of members are relevant to the scheme.

The directors must draw up a circular which explains the effect of the scheme and send it out with every notice calling the meeting. If the notice is given by means of an advertisement, the advertisement must either include the statement or must state where those entitled to attend the meeting may obtain copies of the statement. In particular, the statement must include details of any material interests of the directors of the company, whether these interests are in their capacity as directors or members or otherwise. It must also state the effect of the scheme on the directors' interests and whether that effect is different from the effect on the like interests of other persons.[4] Again, there are criminal penalties for breach of the section. However, a director (or other officer) will not be fined if the failure to comply with the requirements was caused by another director's refusal to

---

1   *Re National Farmers' Union Development Trust Ltd* [1972] 1 WLR 1548, [1973] 1 All ER 135.
2   For example, parties to litigation involving the company: *BAT Industries plc* (unreported), 3 September 1998.
3   *Re RAC Motoring Services Ltd* [2000] 1 BCLC 307.
4   Companies Act 1985, s 426(2).

supply relevant information and, if this is the case, the director who refuses is liable to be fined.

If the nature of the directors' interests changes between the circulation of the statement and the meeting, the court will decide whether, had a reasonable person been given the revised details, he would have changed his mind as to how to vote. If a reasonable person would have been influenced in this way by the changed circumstances, the court may refuse to approve the scheme.[1]

6.8.3   The meeting to approve or reject the scheme

At the meeting the scheme is put to the vote of the members and is considered approved if a simple majority in number representing three-fourths 'in value' of the members present and voting either in person or by proxy at the meeting agree to it.[2]

In the *NFU* case,[3] the court was faced with deciding how to apply this test in the case of a company limited by guarantee: what does 'in value' mean where there are no shares with a face value? In the case, The NFU Development Trust Limited, a company limited by guarantee, had a membership composed of The NFU Development Company Limited, and 94,000 farmers, farm companies and retired farmers. In the case of certain fundamental constitutional decisions, such as altering the memorandum or articles, The NFU Development Company Limited had weighted voting rights. The memorandum required an initial small contribution from a member as an admission fee, but then no further contributions. There could be no distributions to members while the company continued in business, but on winding up there was a provision which would have entitled every member to a share of any surplus. In order to cut administrative expenses, the directors of the company proposed that the company's membership should be reduced to seven. The court held that because of the possibility, however unlikely, of receiving a share of profits on a winding up of the company, each member had the same financial stake in the company, and so the votes should be counted for the purpose of the section as if each member had owned one share. In other words, the fact that The NFU Development Company Limited had weighted voting rights was not relevant because it was not treated any differently in the winding up distribution provision. (Although in evidence one of the members stated that the theoretical possibility of receiving money on a winding up was less important to him than his right to a vote.)

It is not clear how the court would approach the case of a company in which a member cannot be said to have a stake in the company, for example if the surplus on distribution is to be paid to a charity. Probably if the company

---

1   *Re Minster Assets plc* [1985] BCLC 200.
2   Companies Act 1985, s 425(2).
3   *Re National Farmers' Union Development Trust Ltd* [1972] 1 WLR 1548, [1973] 1 All ER 135.

adopted the 'one member, one vote' principle then the court would regard three-quarters of the votes as three-quarters 'in value'. However, weighted voting rights may be designed to reflect differing financial or other contributions from the members; in these circumstances does each member have an equal stake in the company?

6.8.4   Approval of the scheme by the court

If the court approves the scheme, it binds all the members of the company, or the relevant class as the case may be, once an office copy of the court order is received at Companies House. The company and its officers are obliged to annex a copy of the order to every copy of the memorandum issued after the order is made, and may be fined in the event of default.[1]

If the scheme involves the transfer of the whole or any part of the undertaking or property of any company to another company,[2] the burden of proving that the scheme is fair is heavier than in the case of other schemes.[3] In the *NFU* case, the court refused to sanction the scheme to deprive all the members of their rights, holding that it was something which 'no member voting in the interests of the members as a whole could reasonably approve'. The court rejected the argument of Counsel that since the members could not receive benefits from the company while it was in business, extinguishing the members' rights was reasonable if those rights were impeding the exercise of the objects. However, it was implicit in the court's decision that it would, in principle, be possible to remove an individual as a member in the course of a scheme.

6.8.5   Further powers of the court

If the court does find this burden satisfied then it has some additional powers, set out in s 427 of the Companies Act 1985. These include powers to:

–   effect the transfer of property or liabilities;
–   to provide for the allotting of shares, debentures, or policies in the transferee company;
–   to provide for the dissolution of the transferor company without winding up; and
–   to provide for 'such incidental, consequential and supplemental matters as are necessary to secure that the reconstruction or amalgamation is fully and effectively carried out'.

The court order must be registered at Companies House.[4]

---

1   Companies Act 1985, s 425(3) and (4).
2   Note that the definition of company for s 427 of the Companies Act 1985 will exclude certain very old companies: see s 735(1).
3   *Re Hellenic & General Trust Ltd* [1976] 1 WLR 123.
4   Companies Act 1985, s 427(5).

6.8.6   Registered social landlords

In the case of a company which is a registered social landlord, schemes of arrangement are used to effect consolidations of companies and the court order is not effective unless the Housing Corporation's consent is obtained.[1]

6.9   DISSOLUTION UNDER THE COMPANIES ACT 1985, s 652A

Section 652A of the Companies Act 1985 allows the directors of a company that is not trading and is no longer required to apply to the registrar of companies to have the name of the company removed from the register. This procedure is suitable only for the final dissolution of the company after all its affairs have been dealt with and, most importantly, if it has no remaining assets of any kind, as any assets held by the company become Crown property after the dissolution.

The application is made on form 652A, which must be signed by a majority of the directors and accompanied by a £10 fee. Within seven days after making the application, the directors making the application must deliver or post a copy of the application to all members, employees, creditors, directors who did not sign the application and managers of employee pension funds of the company. The application must also be copied to any person who falls into one of these categories in the three-month period after the application date.

The registrar of companies will place a notice in the London or Edinburgh Gazette, and if there are no objections, the company will be struck off after three months from the date of the notice. In practice, if the application is made in proper circumstances, the most likely objection will be from the Inland Revenue which is concerned to see that all tax has been paid and all returns properly made.

An important feature of s 652A is that the liability of the company's officers continues after the date of dissolution. This does not mean that they become liable for things for which they were not liable before dissolution, but it does mean that if, for example, there has been any breach of the companies legislation, the fact that the company is dissolved does not protect the directors. In addition, a person to whom a copy of the company's application was required to have been given may apply for the restoration of the company to the register at any time within 20 years after dissolution. The company must, therefore, deal adequately with all its debts and liabilities before making the application.

---

1   Housing Act 1996, s 7 and Sch 1, para 13.

The procedure cannot be used if, in the previous three months, the company has changed its name, traded, disposed of any trading asset for value, or engaged in any other activity except doing anything in connection with: the s 652A procedure, concluding the affairs of the company, complying with a statutory requirement, or discharging a liability of the company. These conditions also apply after the application until the date of dissolution, so if the company trades in that period, the application for striking-off must be withdrawn.

Failure to comply with the requirements of s 652A is an offence punishable by a fine, although there is a defence if the accused was not aware of the application or if he took all reasonable steps to perform the duty. The fines may be up to £5,000 if tried by magistrates or unlimited if tried in the Crown Court. In addition, if the directors do not give the copies of the application required by the Companies Act 1985, and this is done with the intention of concealing the application for striking-off, the penalty is up to seven years imprisonment plus a fine. There is also an offence committed if a false application is made. Finally, a conviction may lead to disqualification from being a director or from being involved in the management of a company within the UK for up to 15 years.

APPENDICES

Appendix A

MEMORANDUM AND ARTICLES OF ASSOCIATION[1]

The memorandum and articles set out below are suitable for a not-for-profit company limited by guarantee that is not to be registered as a charity, registered social landlord or to have any other special status. Optional clauses as indicated in the footnotes to this precedent are included as Appendix A1, A2 and A3.

Information to be inserted or alternative wording is given in square brackets.

THE COMPANIES ACTS 1985 & 1989

COMPANY LIMITED BY GUARANTEE

MEMORANDUM OF ASSOCIATION

OF

[*Name of Company*]

1. The name of the Company is "[*Name of Company*]".

2. The registered office of the Company is in [England and Wales].

3. The objects for which the Company is established are: [*insert objects*] ("the Objects").

4. The Company has power to do anything within the law that may promote or may help to promote the Objects or any of them. In particular (but without limitation) the Company has the following powers:

    4.1. to pay out of the Company's funds the costs incurred in forming the Company;

    4.2. to acquire or hire property of any kind, and any interests in or rights over property of any kind;

---

1   The author has adapted, with permission, some of the clauses from Jordans Standard Memorandum and Articles of Association for a company limited by guarantee.

4.3. to acquire the whole or any part of the business or assets of any person, firm, or company carrying on any activity in support of the Objects and to give any form of consideration in return for the business or assets;

4.4. to borrow and raise money in any manner; and to secure and guarantee by any means the repayment of any money borrowed, raised or owing, and the performance by the Company of any obligation or liability, by mortgage, charge, standard security, lien or other security upon the whole or any part of the Company's property or assets (whether present or future);

4.5. to invest and deal with the moneys of the Company not immediately required in any manner and to hold or otherwise deal with any investments made;

4.6. to sell, dispose of, let, mortgage, or charge any property of the Company and to grant licences, options, rights and privileges in respect of, or otherwise deal with, all or any part of the property and rights of the Company;

4.7. to make grants or loans of money and to give guarantees and indemnities on any terms; and to support and subscribe to any charitable or public object;

4.8. to promote any other company for the purpose of acquiring the whole or any part of the business or property or undertaking or any of the liabilities of the Company, or of undertaking any business or operations which (in the opinion of the Directors) is likely to assist or benefit the Company; and to subscribe for or otherwise acquire all or any part of the shares or securities of any such company;

4.9. to act as agent or broker or trustee for any person, firm or company, and to undertake and perform any form of contract;

4.10. to reward any person, firm or company rendering services to the Company by cash payment or by any other means;

4.11. to set up, establish, support and maintain superannuation and other funds or schemes (whether contributory or non-contributory) for the benefit of any of the employees of the Company or of any subsidiary, holding company or fellow subsidiary of the Company and of their spouses, children and other relatives and dependants; and to lend money to any such employees or to trustees on their behalf to enable any such schemes to be established or maintained;

4.12. to pay out of the Company's funds premiums on insurance policies to cover the liability of the Directors which, by virtue of any rule of law, would otherwise attach to them in respect of any negligence, default, breach of duty or breach of trust of which they may be guilty in relation to the Company: provided that any such insurance or indemnity must not extend to any claim arising from criminal neglect or deliberate default on their part;

4.13.   to amalgamate with or support any other company or undertaking whose objects may (in the opinion of the Directors of the Company) advantageously be combined with the Objects;

4.14.   to sell or otherwise dispose of the whole or any part of the business or property of the Company, either together or in portions, and to accept anything of value in return; and

4.15.   to do all or any of the things or matters permitted by this Memorandum of Association in any part of the world, and as principal, agent, contractor or otherwise, and by or through agents, brokers, sub-contractors or otherwise and either alone or in conjunction with others.

5.   The income and capital of the Company must be applied solely towards the promotion of the Objects. No part of the income or capital may be paid or transferred, directly or indirectly, to the members of the Company, whether by way of dividend or bonus or in any other way that amounts to a distribution of profit or surplus. This does not prevent the payment of:

5.1.   reasonable and proper remuneration to any officer, employee, or member of the Company in return for any services provided to the Company;

5.2.   [discounts provided to members in respect of their purchase of goods or services provided by the Company;]

5.3.   a reasonable rate of interest on money lent to the Company;

5.4.   reasonable rent for property let to the Company;

5.5.   expenses to any officer, employee or member of the Company; or

5.6.   premiums on the indemnity insurance referred to in clause 4.12.

6.   The liability of the members is limited.

7.   If the Company is wound up while a person is a member or within one year after that person ceases to be a member, every member of the Company will contribute such amount as may be required not exceeding £1 to the assets of the Company, for payment of the Company's debts and liabilities accrued before the member ceases to be a member, and of the costs and expenses of winding up, and for the adjustment of the rights of the contributories among themselves.

8.   This clause applies on the winding up or dissolution of the Company. If there is any property of the Company remaining after all the Company's debts and liabilities have been paid or satisfied, it must not be paid or transferred to any or all of the members of the Company. Instead it must be paid or transferred to one or more companies, organisations or institutions that exist for purposes similar to the Objects, each of which has restrictions in its constitution or governing instrument on the distribution of profits and surpluses that are as least as restrictive as those in this Memorandum of Association. The companies, organisations or institutions will be nominated by the directors of the Company and approved

by the members of the Company at or before the winding up or dissolution. If the directors are unable to identify any similar companies, organisations or institutions then they may pay or transfer the surplus to any charity or charities.

9.   Expressions defined in the Articles of Association have the same meanings in this Memorandum of Association.

We, the persons whose names are written below, wish to be formed into a Company under this Memorandum of Association.

[*Insert names, addresses, and signatures of subscribers, with witnesses' names, addresses and signatures.*]

THE COMPANIES ACTS 1985 & 1989

COMPANY LIMITED BY GUARANTEE

ARTICLES OF ASSOCIATION

OF

[Name of Company]

INTERPRETATION

1.   In these Articles:

"the Act" means the Companies Act 1985 or any statutory re-enactment or modification of it;

"AGM" means an annual General Meeting of the Company;

"the Board" means the board of Directors of the Company, acting collectively;

"clear days" in relation to a period of notice means that period excluding the day on which the notice is given or is deemed to have been given, and the day for which the notice is given or on which it is to take effect;

"Director" means a director of the Company acting individually;

"Member" means a member of the Company [except in articles 40–46];

"Memorandum" means the memorandum of association of the Company;

"Objects" means the objects of the Company as set out in the Memorandum from time to time;

"Secretary" means any person appointed to perform the duties of the Secretary of the Company;

expressions referring to writing include references to printing, fax, e-mail and other methods of representing or reproducing words in a visible form;

unless the context otherwise requires, words or expressions contained in these Articles bear the meanings given to them in the Act;

references in these Articles to 'he' or 'him' include male and female individuals and corporations.

ADMISSION OF MEMBERS

2.   The company must keep a register of members as required by the Act. The members are:

2.1.   the subscribers to the Memorandum and Articles of Association;

2.2.   [the Directors;][1] and

2.3.   individuals or organisations who apply for admission, are admitted as members by the Board, and, (if stated in the application for membership) pay a subscription. Every application for membership must be in one of the forms set out in Article 50 or another form approved by the Board. At the next meeting of the Board (or any committee of the Board established for the purposes of considering applications for admission) after the receipt of any application for membership, the application must be considered by the Board (or committee) who must decide whether to admit or reject the applicant. The Directors are not required to give reasons for their decision.

RETIREMENT OF MEMBERS

3.   A member will cease to be a member:

3.1.   if he resigns by giving notice to the Company;

3.2.   (if the member is a Director) on ceasing to be a Director for whatever reason;

3.3.   if an individual, upon death, or if he becomes of unsound mind, or is convicted of any indictable offence for which he is sentenced to a term of imprisonment;

3.4.   in any case, if any subscription or membership fee due to the Company remains outstanding for more than one month; or

3.5.   (except in the case of a Director) if he is removed from the membership in accordance with any Rule established from time to time pursuant to Article 47.

No member of the Company is entitled to any refund of subscription or membership fee on ceasing to be a member for any reason. Membership of the Company is not transferable.[2]

GENERAL MEETINGS

4.   The Company must hold a general meeting in each year as its AGM, in addition to any other meetings held in that year. The interval between the date of one AGM and the date of the next must not be more than 15 months. The Board will choose the time and place of the AGM. All general meetings of the Company other than AGMs are called Extraordinary General Meetings.

---

1   Directors need not be members of the company unless this is required by the Articles. This Article makes the directors automatically members of the company; see also Articles 3.2 and 3.5.

2   See Appendix A3(ii).

5. The Board may call a general meeting at any time; and must call a general meeting if it receives a requisition by the members of the Company in accordance with the Act.

6. An AGM and a meeting called for the passing of a special resolution must be called by at least 21 clear days' notice, and all other general meetings must be called by at least 14 clear days' notice. A meeting of the Company may be called by shorter notice[1] if it is so agreed:

   6.1. in the case of an AGM, by all the members entitled to attend and vote at that meeting; and

   6.2. in the case of any other meeting, by members holding at least 95% of the total voting rights at that meeting of all the members.

7. The notice must specify the place, date and time of the meeting, and the general nature of all items of the business to be transacted; and must, in the case of an AGM, specify the meeting as an AGM. The text of all special, extraordinary and elective resolutions to be proposed at the meeting must be set out in the notice.

8. Notice must be given to the members of the Company, to the Directors, and to the auditors; but if anyone entitled to receive notice does not receive it, this does not invalidate the proceedings at the meeting if the failure to notify was accidental.

PROCEEDINGS AT GENERAL MEETINGS

9. A general meeting is not valid unless a quorum of members of the Company is present throughout the meeting; the quorum is one half of the members of the Company or two members of the Company (whichever is the greater) present in person or by proxy.

10. If a quorum is not present within half an hour after the time set for the meeting, the meeting is automatically adjourned to the same day in the next week, at the same time and place, or to another day, time and place decided by the Board.

11. The Chairman of the Board will preside as Chairman of every general meeting of the Company. If there is no Chairman of the Board, or if he is not present within fifteen minutes after the time appointed set for the meeting, or is unwilling to act, those Directors present at the meeting must elect one of themselves to be Chairman of the meeting.

12. If at any general meeting no Director is willing to act as Chairman, or if no Director is present within fifteen minutes after the time set for the meeting, the members of the Company present must choose one of themselves to be Chairman of the meeting.

---

1 The provisions of s 369 of the Companies Act 1985 relating to short notice apply whatever is stated in the Articles. However, short notice provisions may be redundant in the case of a company with a very large membership and they may be omitted from the Articles.

13. The Chairman may adjourn the meeting with the consent of any quorate meeting (and must if required by a simple majority of the members present at the meeting), but no business may be transacted at any adjourned meeting other than the business left unfinished at the meeting from which the adjournment took place. No notice is required of an adjourned meeting unless the meeting is adjourned for 30 days or more, in which case notice must be given as in the case of the original meeting.

14. At any general meeting, a resolution put to the vote of the meeting will be decided on a show of hands unless a poll is demanded (before or on the declaration of the result of the show of hands). Subject to the Act, a poll may be demanded:

    14.1. by the Chairman; or

    14.2. by at least two members of the Company present in person or by proxy; or

    14.3. by any member or members of the Company present in person or by proxy and representing not less than 10% of the total voting rights of all the members of the Company having the right to vote at the meeting.

15. Unless a poll is demanded, a declaration by the Chairman that a resolution has been carried or lost on a show of hands, whether unanimously or by a particular majority, and an entry to that effect in the minutes, is conclusive evidence of the fact, without proof of the number or proportion of the votes recorded in favour of or against the resolution.

16. The demand for a poll may be withdrawn before the poll is taken, but only with the consent of the Chairman. The withdrawal of a demand for a poll does not invalidate the result of a show of hands declared before the demand for the poll is made.

17. Except as provided in Article 18, if a poll is demanded it may be taken in such manner as the Chairman directs but the Chairman has no authority in exercising this power to extend the poll to members of the Company who are not present at the meeting in question. The result of the poll is deemed to be the resolution of the meeting at which the poll was demanded.

18. A poll demanded on the election of a Chairman, or on a question of adjournment of a meeting, must be taken immediately. A poll demanded on any other question may be taken at such time as the Chairman directs. If there is an interval before the time for closing the poll, the meeting may deal with any business other than the business being determined by poll.

VOTES OF MEMBERS

19. Every member of the Company whose name is entered in the Company's register of members has one vote at every general meeting. A resolution proposed at any general meeting will be approved if at least one half of the

votes cast at the meeting are in favour of the resolution, except where the Act or these Articles prescribes a different majority.

PROXIES AND REPRESENTATIVES

20. A member of the Company may appoint a proxy to attend general meetings in his place and to vote on a poll [but not on a show of hands]. The proxy form must be in writing in the form set out in Article 51 (one-way proxy form) or 52 (two-way proxy form) or as near to one of those forms as possible, and signed by the member or by another person under a power of attorney granted by a member. In the case of a member which is a company, the proxy form must be in writing and signed by two directors or a director and the secretary of that company. A proxy need not be a member of the Company.

21. The proxy form (and the power of attorney, if any, under which it is signed, or a copy of that power certified by a solicitor) must be deposited at the registered office of the Company, or at another place within the United Kingdom specified for that purpose in the notice convening the meeting, not less than 48 hours before the time set for the meeting or adjourned meeting in question; or, in the case of a poll, not less than twenty four hours before the time appointed for the taking of the poll. If this Article is not complied with the proxy form is invalid.

22. A vote given or poll demanded by a proxy for a member, or by the authorised representative of a member which is an organisation remains valid despite the previous revocation of the authority of proxy or representative unless notice of revocation was received by the Company at its registered office before the start of the meeting or adjourned meeting in question.

DIRECTORS[1]

23. The first Directors of the Company are those named in the statement submitted to the registrar of companies on incorporation of the Company. At the first AGM, all the Directors must retire from office unless the members of the Company do not appoint or re-appoint at least one Director at that meeting in which case they will all remain in office. At every subsequent AGM, one-third of the Directors then in office must retire. If the number of Directors is not divisible by three, then the number nearest to one-third must retire. A Director who retires by rotation is eligible for reappointment if he is willing to continue to act as Director.

24. The Directors to retire by rotation are those who have been longest in office since their last appointment or re-appointment; but as between Directors who were last appointed or re-appointed on the same day, the

---

1   Note that in these Articles there are no provisions authorising the appointment of alternates; but an equivalent of the Table A provisions may be included.

Board must draw lots to determine who is to retire, unless the Directors in question agree the order of retirement among themselves.

25. If the members of the company do not fill the vacancy left by a Director who retires by rotation the retiring Director will, if willing to act, be deemed to have been re-appointed unless at the meeting it is resolved not to fill the vacancy or unless a resolution for the re-appointment of the Director is put to the meeting and lost.

26. No person other than a Director retiring by rotation may be appointed or re-appointed as a Director at any general meeting unless:

    26.1. he is recommended by the Directors; or

    26.2. at least 28 clear days before the date appointed for the meeting, notice executed by a member of the Company qualified to vote at the meeting has been given to the Company of the intention to propose that person for appointment or re-appointment, together with notice executed by that person of his willingness to be appointed or re-appointed.

27. A notice of a general meeting of the Company must include the name of any person (other than a Director retiring by rotation at the meeting) who is recommended by the Board for appointment or re-appointment as a Director at the meeting, or in respect of whom notice has been duly given to the Company under Article 26.2 above.

28. The Company may by ordinary resolution appoint as a Director a person who is willing to act, either to fill a vacancy or as an additional Director; and may also determine the order of rotation of any additional Directors.

29. The Board may co-opt as a Director a person who is willing to act, either to fill a vacancy or as an additional Director. A Director co-opted by the Board under this Article will hold office only until the next following AGM, and will not be taken into account in determining the Directors who are to retire by rotation at that meeting. If a co-opted Director is not re-appointed at that AGM, he will automatically vacate office at the end of the meeting.

30. A technical defect in the appointment of a Director does not invalidate a decision taken at a Board meeting if the Directors present were not aware of the defect at the time of the meeting.

31. A Director will cease to be a Director:

    31.1. if he resigns his directorship by giving notice to the Company;

    31.2. upon death, or if he becomes bankrupt or makes any arrangement with his creditors, or becomes of unsound mind, or is convicted of an indictable offence for which he is sentenced to a term of imprisonment;

    31.3. if he is removed by a simple majority of the members of the Company, following the procedure laid down in Section 303 of the Act; or

31.4. if he is disqualified under the Company Directors Disqualification Act 1986 or otherwise.

32. The Board has control over all the affairs and property of the Company, and may exercise all the powers of the Company, except as otherwise provided by the Memorandum of Association of the Company and these Articles, or by any Rules made pursuant to Article 47. Every Director has one vote at a Board meeting.

33. A Director may call a Board meeting at any time and the Secretary must call a Board meeting if requested to do so by a Director. The Board may convene and regulate its meetings as it thinks fit. Questions arising at any Board meeting will be decided by a majority of votes.

34. A Board meeting is not valid unless a quorum is present throughout the meeting. The quorum is one Director if there is a sole Director in office, but otherwise is one half of the Directors then holding office or two Directors (whichever is the greater).[1]

35. The Chairman of the Board will preside at every Board meeting. If at any Board meeting the Chairman is not present within fifteen minutes after the time set for the start of the meeting, the Directors present must choose one of their number to be Chairman of the meeting. In the case of an equality of votes on any question the Chairman has a second or casting vote.

36. The Board may delegate any of its powers to a managing director and to committees consisting of such Directors, members of the Company and others as it thinks fit: in the exercise of the delegated powers, any managing director or committee must conform to any regulations which may be imposed by the Directors or by Rules made under Article 47.

BENEFITS TO DIRECTORS

37. The Directors are entitled to receive such remuneration, expenses, and other benefits as the Board determines.

SECRETARY

38. The Company must have a Secretary who will be appointed by the Board on whatever terms the Board thinks fit. If there is no Secretary capable of acting, anything required or authorised to be done by or to the Secretary may be done by any Director authorised generally, or specially for that purpose, by the Board.

---

1 In these Articles there are no saving provisions allowing a director to vote in a matter in which he is interested. It may be necessary to include these provisions if the board is very small and the company is likely to do a lot of business with directors or with their other companies.

SEAL

39. The Company is not required to have a common seal. If the Company has a common seal, it may only be used by the authority of the Board. Every document bearing an impression of the common seal must be signed by a Director, and countersigned by the Secretary or by a second Director.

NOTICES, MEETINGS AND RESOLUTIONS

40. The following Articles 41 to 46 apply to meetings and resolutions of, and notices given to, the Board, committees of the Board, and the Company in general meeting; and "member" means a Director, committee member or a member of the Company in general meeting as the context requires.

41. Any notice to be given under these Articles must be in writing. The Company may give any notice to a member by handing it to him personally, or by sending it by post (airmail in the case of overseas members who have given no address for service within the United Kingdom) in a prepaid envelope addressed to the member at the address shown in the Company's register of members, or by leaving it at that address. Where the member has given to the Company a fax number or e-mail address to which notices may be sent electronically, the Company may give a valid notice by means of fax or e-mail.

42. A member present in person at any meeting is taken to have received notice of the meeting and, where necessary, of the purposes for which it was called.

43. Proof that an envelope containing a notice was properly addressed, prepaid and posted shall be conclusive evidence that the notice was given to a postal address. Electronic confirmation of receipt shall be conclusive evidence that a notice was given to a facsimile number or e-mail address. A notice is deemed to be given at the expiration of 48 hours after it was handed to the member, posted or (as the case may be) transmitted by fax or e-mail.

44. Subject to the provisions of the Act (and in particular in the case of a resolution of the members of the Company, to any requirement to submit the proposed resolution to the auditors), a resolution in writing signed by all the members entitled to attend and vote at a meeting is as valid and effective as if it had been passed at a meeting properly convened and held. Any resolution in writing may consist of two or more documents in similar form, each signed by one or more members. Digital signatures and faxed signatures will suffice for the purpose of this Article.[1]

---

1   Provisions of the Articles permitting electronic communications may not be necessary after implementation of orders made under the Electronic Communications Act 2000.

45. A member entitled to attend and vote at a meeting may participate by means of a telephone conference or other facility enabling all people participating in the meeting to hear each other; and participation in a meeting in this manner is taken to be presence in person at the meeting.

46. The Secretary or a Director must take minutes of proceedings at all meetings, and the minutes must be authenticated and kept in accordance with the requirements of the Act.

RULES

47. The Directors may establish Rules for any purposes required from time to time for the effective operation of the Company or the furtherance of the Objects, including the levying of annual subscriptions or membership fees; provided that if there is a conflict between the terms of these Articles or the Memorandum of Association of the Company and any Rules established under this Article, the terms of the Memorandum and Articles will prevail.

INDEMNITY

48. Subject to the Act, but without affecting any indemnity to which he may otherwise be entitled, every Director and every officer of the Company, will be indemnified out of the assets of the Company against any liability incurred by him in defending any proceedings, whether civil or criminal, alleging liability for negligence, default, breach of duty or breach of trust in relation to the affairs of the Company, and in which judgment is given in his favour, or in which he is acquitted, or in connection with any application in which relief is granted to him by the Court.

49. Subject to the Act, the Company may purchase and maintain for any Director or for any officer of the Company, insurance cover against any liability which may attach to him by virtue of any rule of law in respect of any negligence, default, breach of duty or breach of trust of which he or she may be guilty in relation to the Company, and against all costs, charges, losses, expenses and liabilities incurred by him and for which he is entitled to be indemnified by the Company under Article 48.

FORMS[1]

50. The forms of the application for membership referred to in Article 2 are as follows.

    In the case of an individual:

---

1   It is more conventional to place these in the body of the Articles but positioning them at the end may assist the company if it has an electronic copy of the Articles and wishes to cut and paste the relevant form.

To the Board of [*name of Company*]

I, [*name*]
of [*address*]

wish to become a member of [*name of Company*], subject to the provisions
of the Memorandum and Articles of Association of the Company and to
the Rules. I agree to pay to the company an amount of up to £1 if the
company is wound up while I am a member or for up to 12 months after I
have left the Company. [*(If appropriate:)* I agree to pay a subscription of
[*amount*] on [*date*], and to pay any membership fee levied in accordance
with the Company's Rules.]

Signature: ....

Date: ....

In the case of an organisation:

To the Board of [*name of Company*]

[*name of Organisation*] whose registered office/principal place of business
is at [*address of registered office/principal place of business*] applies for
membership of [*name of Company*], subject to the provisions of the
Memorandum and Articles of Association of the Company and to
the Rules. It agrees to pay to the company an amount of up to £1 if the
company is wound up while it is a member or for up to 12 months after it
has left the Company. [*(If appropriate:)* It agrees to pay a subscription of
[*amount*] on [*date*], and to pay any membership fee levied in accordance
with the Company's Rules.]

Authorised

Signature: ....

Name: ....

Position: ....

Date: ....

51. The one-way proxy form referred to in Article 20 is as follows:

[*Name of Company*]

I, [*name*]
of [*address*]

being a member of the above Company, appoint [*name of proxy*]
of [*address of proxy*]
or failing him/her [*name of alternative proxy*]
of [*address of alternative proxy*]
as my proxy to vote for me on my behalf at the General Meeting of the
Company to be held on [*date*] and at any adjournment, and to join in any
demand for a poll in accordance with the Articles.

Signed: ....

Date: ....

52. The two-way proxy form referred in Article 20 is as follows:

[*Name of Company*]

I, [*name*]
of [*address*]
being a member of the above Company, appoint [*name of proxy*]
of [*address of proxy*]
or failing him/her [*name of alternative proxy*]
of [*address of alternative proxy*]
as my proxy to vote for me on my behalf at the Annual/Extraordinary*
General Meeting of the Company to be held on [*date*] and at any
adjournment, and to join in any demand for a poll in accordance with the
Articles.

Signed: ....

Date: ....

This form is to be used *in favour of/against the resolution.

Unless otherwise instructed, the proxy will vote as he/she thinks fit.

* Strike out whichever you do not want.

We, the persons whose names are written below, wish to be formed into a
Company under these Articles of Association:

[*Insert names, addresses, and signatures of subscribers, with witnesses' names,
addresses and signatures.*]

Appendix A1

ALTERNATIVE CLAUSES FOR A PROPERTY MANAGEMENT COMPANY

Memorandum

Clause 3: insert in definition of the Objects

To acquire, develop, manage, deal with and administer the freehold or leasehold property or properties known as [*name of Estate*] ("the Estate"), together with services, facilities and amenities of every description in relation to the Estate.

Articles

Additional definitions:

"the Estate" has the meaning given in clause [3] of the Memorandum;

"Dwelling" means any residential unit in the Estate;

"Tenant" means the person or persons to whom a lease or tenancy of a Dwelling has been granted;

Version 1: a company to manage an existing block or estate

Article 2: substitute the following:

The company must keep a register of members as required by the Act. The subscribers to the Memorandum are the first members. Apart from the subscribers, only Tenants will be admitted as members. The Company must accept as a member every person who is a Tenant and who has complied with this Article. Every member other than the subscribers must sign a written consent to become a member. If two or more persons are together one Tenant they must each sign a written consent, but they will together count as one member. The person whose name appears first in the register of members will be entitled to exercise the voting powers of that member.

Article 3: substitute the following:

Each subscriber to the Memorandum who is not a Tenant will automatically cease to be a member as soon as Tenants for all the Dwellings have become members. A Tenant may not resign as a member while holding (either alone or jointly with others) a legal estate in a Dwelling. A Tenant will automatically cease to be a member on the registration of a successor to his Dwelling as a member. If a member dies or becomes bankrupt, his personal representatives or trustee in bankruptcy will be entitled to be registered as a member if he is or they are a Tenant.

Version 2: Enhanced voting rights for the developer of a new estate or block

Article 2: substitute the following:

The company must keep a register of members as required by the Act. The subscribers to the memorandum are the first members. A subscriber may nominate any person to succeed him as a member and his nominee (unless he is or becomes a Tenant) has the same power to nominate his own successor. Apart from the subscribers and nominated successors, only Tenants will be admitted as members. The Company must accept as a member every person who is a Tenant and who has complied with this Article. Every member other than the subscribers must sign a written consent to become a member. If two or more persons are together one Tenant they must each sign a written consent, but they will together count as one member. The person whose name appears first in the register of members will be entitled to exercise the voting powers of that member.

Article 3: substitute the following:

Each subscriber to the memorandum (and each nominated successor) who is not a Tenant will automatically cease to be a member as soon as Tenants for all the Dwellings have become members.

Article 19: substitute the following:

Every member present in person or by proxy or (if a corporation) by an authorised representative has one vote at a general meeting. However, if no Tenant exists in respect of any Dwelling, the subscribers to the Memorandum or their nominated successors under article 2 will have three votes in respect of every Dwelling in addition to their own votes as members, whether the voting is by means of a show of hands or a poll. If there is more than one subscriber or successor, their extra votes will be held jointly.

Appendix A2

OPTIONAL CLAUSES FOR THE EXPULSION OF A MEMBER

Articles

Add to Article 47:

No Rule as to the manner in which a member may be removed from membership of the Company is valid unless it provides that the member is to be given an opportunity to be heard at any meeting at which the question of removal is to be determined.

Rules or Articles (Articles should always have numbered paragraphs):

Any member of the Company may be removed from membership in accordance with the following rules but by no other method.

A member may be removed if, in the opinion of the Board, he has acted or has threatened to act in a manner which is contrary to the interests of the Company as a whole or if his conduct (whether as a member or otherwise) is likely to bring the Company, or any or all of its Directors or members into disrepute.

If at a meeting of the Board a resolution is passed to remove a member, the Board must serve a notice on the member stating that the Board has resolved to invoke the provisions of these rules [and giving a statement of the reasons for the Board's decision. The statement of reasons must be sufficiently detailed in the circumstances to enable the member to know the case against him].

The notice to the member must also give the member the opportunity to make representations to the Board [in writing] [or in person at a mutually convenient time] as to why he should not be removed as a member. The Board must consider any representations made by the member and, if the representations are not made by the member at a Board meeting, the Board must consider the representations at the next Board meeting.

After the Board meeting at which the representations are considered, the Board must serve a notice on the member informing him of the decision. If the decision is to remove the member, this must be reflected in the register of members as soon as reasonably practicable.

There will be no right of appeal from a decision of the Board to remove a member. After the removal of the member has been noted in the register of members he will have no right to attend and vote at general meetings of the Company and he will cease to be entitled to any other benefits of membership.

He will [not] be entitled to a refund of any subscription, membership fee or joining fee paid by him for his membership of the Company.

The Board's proceedings and the statement of reasons for removal will be confidential and the Board must make no statement to the other members of the Company concerning the member's removal unless the member himself chooses to make public the issue of his removal, or to make it a matter of interest to the members of the Company as a whole.

Appendix A3

MISCELLANEOUS CLAUSES

A3(i) Incorporating a club

Article 2: add the following:

2.4 every person who at the date of incorporation of the Company was a member of the unincorporated association known as [*name of club*], and who within [ ] months after incorporation, deposits at the registered office a written election to become a member.

A3(ii) Transfer of membership

Article 2: add the following:

A member may transfer his membership rights and privileges by signing a document in writing and depositing it at the registered office of the Company. The Board must promptly register the name of the transferee in the register of members and must notify the transferee of the date on which it was admitted to membership.

A3(iii) Death of a member

Article 3.3: delete the reference to the death of a member and add:

On the death of a member, one of his personal representatives is entitled, with the approval of the Board, to succeed to the rights of membership himself, or to transfer them to another person.

A3(iii) Postal ballots

Additional clause:

The Board may resolve that any matter which these articles permit the Company to deal with by means of an ordinary resolution, and is not required by the Act to be dealt with by the Company in general meeting, may be determined by a postal ballot to be conducted in a manner determined by the Board. Any resolution declared by the Board to have been passed by a simple majority of the members of the Company who cast votes for or against the resolution in the ballot, has effect as if it were an ordinary resolution of the Company passed at a properly convened and properly conducted meeting.

A3(iv) Entrenched weighted voting rights in the memorandum

Additional clause:

On a resolution to alter [the memorandum]/[the articles]/[specific provisions], [*name*] and [*name*] shall, while they are members of the Company, each have three additional votes for every vote cast by every other member, whether the vote is taken by means of a show of hands or a poll. No alteration may be made to this clause.

Appendix B

CHECKLIST OF DOCUMENTS REQUIRED FOR INCORPORATION

The following documents are required for incorporation by post or personal presentation at Companies House. Shortly it will be possible to file documents electronically and the requirements relating to signature and declaration will be adjusted for submitting documents for incorporation by electronic means.

(1) A printed copy of the memorandum and articles, each of which must be signed by every subscriber in the presence of a witness. Note that, unlike a company limited by shares, a company limited by guarantee cannot file only a memorandum, leaving Table A to be incorporated into the constitution by the Companies Act 1985.

(2) Companies House forms:

Form 10: gives the details of the name of the company, the postal address of the first registered office, the company secretary and the directors. The officers of the company must sign the form. At least one director is required and the sole director may not also be the company secretary. Home addresses must be given. The form may be signed by the subscribers or by an agent (eg a solicitor) on their behalf.

Form 12: this is a statutory declaration sworn by a solicitor engaged in the company formation or by one of the directors of the company, stating that the requirements of the Companies Act 1985 as to formation have been complied with. It will need to be sworn in the presence of a solicitor or other person authorised to take statutory declarations, and a fee will be payable (currently £5).

Form 30(5)(a): this is required only if the company wishes to take advantage of the exemption from using the word 'limited' or its Welsh equivalent in the company name. Again a statutory declaration is required and a fee payable.

(3) Approval required for any sensitive words: see Chapter 2.

(4) Cheque for the incorporation fee, payable to Companies House. The fee is currently £20 for a standard incorporation or £100 for a same-day incorporation.

Companies House addresses (and see also www.companieshouse.gov.uk)

Companies House
Crown Way
Cardiff
CF14 3UZ
DX 33050 Cardiff
Tel: +44 (0)29 2038 8588; Fax: +44 (0)29 2038 0900
Call Centre Tel: +44 (0)29 2038 0801

Companies House
PO BOX 29019
21 Bloomsbury Street
London
WC1B 3XD
Tel: +44 (0)29 2038 0801; Fax: +44 (0)29 2038 0900

Companies House
37 Castle Terrace
Edinburgh
EH1 2EB
Tel: +44 (0)131 535 5800; Fax: +44 (0)131 535 5820

Appendix C

APPLICATION FOR MEMBERSHIP

This precedent includes an application form for membership of a company limited by guarantee, together with a note explaining to a member what a company is and what membership of it means for them. It is particularly designed for the situation where a club is incorporated but may be adapted for other situations.

[NAME OF COMPANY]

[*Name of Company*] is a company limited by guarantee. This means that it does not have shares or shareholders, but instead it has members. Its day-to-day management is carried out by the directors, but by becoming a member you will be entitled to do the following things:

– to attend and vote at general meetings; normally there will be one meeting per year, called the Annual General Meeting or AGM, and you will be given at least three weeks' notice of the place and time of the meeting. We may also need to call other general meetings in exceptional circumstances
– to receive the annual accounts of the company
– to elect directors by voting at the meeting
– to vote on any fundamental changes to the nature of the company, its name, its purposes, or what happens to its profits.

You will not be entitled to receive any dividend or other income from the company.

If the company makes a profit this will be retained to help pay for the company's activities in the following years. If the company is wound up you will not receive any money from the company because its constitution requires that it should be paid to [*another similar organisation or to a charity*].

The constitution is made up of the memorandum and the articles [and the rules]. The memorandum sets out what the company can do and why it exists; and the articles deal with the holding of meetings, the admission of members, the election of directors and other rules relating to the running of the company. These are legal documents that are registered on the public records for the company held at Companies House. They may also be inspected at [*address*] [, where you may also inspect the rules made by the company to date].

You will not be liable for any debts of the company by becoming a member. You will not be liable if someone brings a legal case against the company. This is because like most other companies it is a limited company, which means your liability as a member is limited. If the company is wound up (which may happen, for example, if it cannot pay its debts) then you will have to pay no more than [£1] to the company. This is the amount that you 'guarantee' or promise to pay to the company by becoming a member, as set out in clause [   ] of the memorandum. In addition, if you have paid a subscription to the company there may not be enough funds left to return to you any of that subscription, even if the winding up happens part way through a membership year.

If you would like to become a member, the procedure is as follows:

[*set out procedure as in articles*]

To the Board of [*name of Company*]

I, [*name*]

of [*address*]

wish to become a member of [*name of Company*], subject to the provisions of the Memorandum and Articles of Association of the Company [and to the Rules]. I agree to pay to the company an amount of up to [£1] if the company is wound up while I am a member or for up to 12 months after I have left the Company. [*(If appropriate:)* I agree to pay a subscription of [*amount*] on [*date*], and to pay any membership fee levied in accordance with the Company's Rules.]

Signed ....

Dated ....

Appendix D

NOTICE OF GENERAL MEETING

[NAME OF COMPANY]

[The annual general meeting]/[An extraordinary general meeting] of the company will be held on [*date*] at [*place*] at [*time*], for the following purposes:

To receive the report of the Chairman
To receive and consider the accounts of the company for the year ended [*date*]
To reappoint [*name of firm*] as the auditors of the company and to authorise the board of directors to fix their remuneration
To appoint directors to replace the following who will retire at the meeting:

[*insert names of retiring directors*]

[(Mr [*Name*] and Ms [*Name*] offer themselves for re-election)]
To appoint new directors
To consider, and if thought fit, pass the following resolutions:

[*Special resolutions should be set out in full here. Ordinary resolutions need not be set out in full but the notice should give a sufficient indication of the nature of the business to be transacted at the meeting.*]

Signed by order of the board:

.... Company Secretary

Date ....

Registered office of the company: [*address*]

A member of the company is entitled to appoint a proxy to attend and [, if a poll is taken,] vote in his place at the meeting. A proxy form is enclosed with this notice. Completed proxy forms must arrive at the registered office not less than 48 hours before the time of the meeting. [A proxy need not be a member of the company.]

Appendix E

CONTENTS OF COMPANY NOTEPAPER

The following must be included on the notepaper:

Full name of company (accurately including or omitting the word limited,[1] its abbreviation ltd, or, for companies incorporated in Wales, the Welsh equivalent or its permitted abbreviation)

Registered in [England and Wales, Scotland or Wales]

Company number

Registered office address

The following may be included:

Trading name or logo

Trading address or address for correspondence

The full names, or surnames and initials, of *all* the directors of the company

The names of the company secretary and other officers

VAT registration number if applicable

There may be additional requirements where the company has a special status. For example, the notepaper of a registered charity should include its charity registration number.

---

1   For a full explanation of this point, see **2.3.7**.

INDEX

References are to paragraph numbers; *italic* numbers are to
Appendix material.